ATTITUDE
The Great Life-Maker

by

Roger F. Vanderlaan

ATTITUDE
The Great Life-Maker

BY
ROGER F. VANDERLAAN

PUBLISHED BY: El Camino Publishers

4010 Calle Real
Suite 4
Santa Barbara, CA 93110

Copyright © 1986 by Roger F. Vanderlaan
First Printing 1986
Printed in the United States of America

Library of Congress Catalog Card No.: 86-80082
Vanderlaan, Roger F. Attitude: Santa Barbara, Ca
El Camino Publishers 230 P.

Library of Congress Cataloging in Publication Data

Vanderlaan, Roger F., 1931 -
    Attitude: the great life-maker.

    Includes index.
    Summary: Defines attitude, defines its various components, and discusses its role in determining what a human being is going to accomplish, become, or stand for during the course of a lifetime.
    1. Attitude (Psychology)   2. Success.
    [1. Attitude (Psychology)   2. Success.   3. Conduct of life]
    I. Title.
BF327.V36 1986   158'.1   86-80082

ISBN 0-942060-01-6 Paperback
ISBN 0-942060-02-4 Hardcover

For Debbie . . .
Whose uncommon courage and fighting spirit have
made me very proud to be her Daddy.

ABOUT THE COVER

The now famous Brooks Institute, School of Photographic Art and Science, Santa Barbara, California, was founded October 1945 by Ernest H. Brooks, a professional photographer who could see that traditional training methods would no longer meet the industry's ever expanding demands. The result of his foresight is one of the world's great schools of professional photography which now has more than 800 students enrolled, representing as many as 35 countries.

Graduates emerge with a Bachelor of Arts Degree, or a Master of Science Degree in professional Photography.

Under the able leadership of Ernest H. Brooks II, who assumed the presidency from his father in 1971, Brooks Institute has continued to be one of the world's foremost schools of photography.

It was to this place of excellence that the Author journeyed in search of an appropriate cover for this book.

A contest was held among the students with cash prizes for the four finalists being donated by Mr. Vanderlaan.

The choice for first place was not easily made, as the versatile talents, and bright imaginations of the students offered up an impressive display of differing approaches.

The winner at last was Tom Skiffington, a former Chicagoan in his third year at Brooks. The photography and the concept that you see on the front cover of this book are his.

El Camino Publishers takes particular pride in wishing Mr. Skiffington the best of everything in the years ahead . . .

We also acknowledge with gratitude, the friendly cooperation shown by Ernest H. Brooks II, and Dick Atamian of Brooks Institute . . . Ed.

TABLE OF CONTENTS

INTRODUCTION

ATTITUDE
THE GREAT LIFE MAKER

There is no question whatsoever that *attitude* is the single, most important factor which will determine what a human being is going to accomplish, become, or stand for during their short stay on this rotund little ball of mud we call earth.

In recent years much has been written and learned about various components of the attitude (such as positive self image) etc. But I must submit to you that I believe these things to be only small pieces of the pie. I am convinced that the more we explore helpful ingredients of our individual makeup, the more we will be made aware that we are dealing with bits and pieces of a larger whole, and when the chips are all in, we will be forced to admit that the thing that probably needs overhauling in most of our lives is —*our attitudes*.

We will be exploring at length the reasons that have led me to this conclusion later on in these pages, but before we go any further, let's take a hard look at *attitude*. What I believe it to be, and why I am persuaded that at this very moment, your own personal attitude is either your worst enemy, your best friend, or a profoundly important aspect of your makeup that needs to be examined thoroughly, the purpose of which is to "know thyself" better.

What Exactly is Attitude?

I have an old copy of "The American College Dictionary" (Random House—1947) upon which I used to sit while getting a haircut. Down in the deepest recesses of my heart, I always knew that some day I would open it, and understand every word in there. Well — maybe some day I will — but not today. I did open it long enough to look up a word though. The word was ATTITUDE. The description of attitude as it pertains to our purposes here was very brief. It said, "Position, disposition, or manner with regard to a person or thing". And the brevity of that explanation pretty well indicates the lack of attention that has been paid to our attitudes, and to the immeasurable impact that they have on our lives. Allow me, if you will, to give my own description of attitude.

ATTITUDE:
Your attitude has caused you to be who and what you are. It is the great *lifemaker*, and be assured that it can either make you or break you. It will be the single most important factor which determines what you will become as a human being, and what your life will be like—or perhaps IS like. It is the barometer of your feelings, it is your overall approach and reaction to everything you think, feel, see and do. It is the *complexion* of your outlook on life. It is (and this is important) a REFLECTION of your true self. Attitude can truly be called "The window of the soul."

The deeper we probe into the reasons and motivations for our actions and reactions, the more we are made aware of the ultra-complexities of our subconscious drives, and the more we begin to understand the reasons for some of our long held beliefs. Under the cold scrutiny of an honest, mature and completely unbiased re-appraisal, we are often shocked to learn just how *wrong* we have been about some things. Nevertheless, it is a road that must be traveled if we are to have any say at all as to what our attitudes will be. The alternative is to accept all of our present attitudes as being correct, no matter how *wrongly* we are programmed to begin with, or by whom.

We can make a comparison between our present attitudes and a computer which has been fed faulty information. Once this input is accepted as fact, it is totally impossible to come up with *right* answers unless and until we re-evaluate the information and then follow up by re-programming the correct information into the computer's memory banks, or in this case, our *attitude banks.*

I must tell you at the outset that as constructive as this may appear to be—it's not easy. Be cognizant of the fact that much of your re-evaluation and your re-programming will be done by your *old computer*. Fortunately, the human brain has a great deal more latitude than even the most sophisticated of computers. You will, however, be making decisions based upon earlier, sometimes erroneous decisions. At a later point in this book we will be looking at the *de-programming* and *re-programming* of our attitudes. For the present, however, let us define the purpose of this book so that we may accomplish something of value here.

You may begin training your attitude to respond to your needs and goals right now, rather than allowing pre-conceived ideas to dominate your thinking. The attitude which you take toward the reading of this book will, in large part, determine "what you will get out of it." I hope that you will consider the thoughts we examine together carefully and after weighing them in an open minded, investigative manner, apply them to your own life, even if you find that somewhat painful in some cases. No truly honest inquiry into "what makes us tick" can be made without opening old wounds and forcing us to admit to unpleasant discoveries about ourselves. We will have to begin by rejecting those things which we suspect to be untrue. No one on God's green earth is thrilled to learn that they have been *wrong* about something. Not you and certainly not I. Be that as it may, we will proceed in the examination of our attitudes with *truth* as our guidepost. You know what I'm saying — if the shoe fits — eat it.

The purpose of this book is threefold.

> ONE. To make you aware of the tremendous, unfathomable effect that your *attitude* has on your life.

> TWO. To show you unimpeachable evidence that you have an extraordinary "super weapon" at your disposal, once you learn to *control* rather than *conform to* your attitude.

> THREE. To show you how to *program* your attitude with favorable, positive information.

CHAPTER ONE

HOW YOU ACQUIRED
YOUR PRESENT ATTITUDE

Your attitude is shaped by the *sum total* of all your experiences, both good and bad. Your own self image (the way you see yourself), the way you think others see you, your feelings about other people, your beliefs, your opinions, your prejudices, your education, your instruction, your parents viewpoints and the attitude of friends and associates with whom you come in contact. Even the very air you breath has in some way effected your attitude. Do you find that difficult to believe? Let me give you an example. I spent a lot of my earlier years in Decatur, Illinois, where my mother and two of my brothers and their families reside to this day. Decatur, Illinois, is the home of *Staleys Manufacturing Company*, a large, complex network of buildings where they process soy beans and other farm products, and make them into useful household items, some of which you probably have in your home today. On certain days, Decatur has the distinct odor of burnt beans. To someone from out of town, this is not a pleasant odor and yet whenever I smell a similar odor, I am immediately whisked back in time, to Mom and Dad and family and pleasant memories, even though I haven't lived there for many years. The point is—one man's *stink* is another man's *pleasant memories*. If you happen to have been raised down wind from the Chicago stockyards, chances are pretty good that you will associate the smell of cattle, sheep and other farm animals with home. If on the other hand, you were raised in say New York City, the possibility of conjuring up pleasant memories from the smell of cow dung are pretty remote. So where one man enjoys the odor and finds himself in a pleasant mood as a result of it, another man may just want to get the hell out of there.

In order to carry this one step farther, supposing you were raised in the deep south where the pace of life is slower and where the long, hot summers slow everyone down to one notch above "stop". Could it be that the smell of magnolia blossoms in bloom, or orange blossoms, would then cause you to slow down no matter where you found yourself? Studies into human behavior patterns seem to indicate that this is a distinct possibility. The subject of orange blossoms reminds me of many years ago when I decided to run away from home and go to Florida. I was a young man at the time without much to offer potential employers in the way of experience. I spent a lot of time looking for a job, and to this day the smell of orange blossoms reminds me of *starvation*.

It is safe to say that **everything** you have ever experienced has in some way contributed to your attitude. And that experiences long forgotten by your conscious mind, still influence your actions today.

Little Things and Little People

If we are to investigate the causes of some of our beliefs, then we must back-track to the point of their origin. This means returning in time to that place of learning where most of our opinions were established long ago when our minds were young and pliable and our hearts accepted as *gospel truth* anything told to us by that special loved one. Perhaps it was at the knee of gra'ma, or maybe on those fishing trips with Dad, or in conversations with a favorite uncle, or a respected neighbor, or family friend. We all had at least one primary *teacher* at the beginning, even though we may not have recognized them as such at that time. For most of us it was Mom or Dad. For many others it was someone we admired and therefore *allowed* to impress us with their viewpoints.

How very difficult it then becomes to *discard* this knowledge when the day comes that we must face the possibility that— *perhaps they were wrong!* It would not be hard for our subconscious mind to confuse an act of learning with an act of disloyalty under those circumstances. You may somehow view your new knowledge as a *violation* of your love for that special person. Obviously the most painless course of action at this juncture, is to take **no** action, and thereby preserve your love and respect for the memory of your teacher. It's a terrible waste, but it's one of the reasons why "old ideas die hard—and slowly".

Permit me, if you will, to illustrate the construction of a *wrong* idea, and to expound somewhat on the possible *long term* complications that can arise as the result of accepting information as valid, based upon your affection for the source of that information rather than your own analytical appraisal.

Ben Taylor

Ben Taylor's uncle was well known all throughout Boon County. He had run a lot of illegal booze in his younger days and the local *wooden bench* boys liked to sit in front of Carsen's General Store and tell stories about the old days when a fast car and a few good connections could earn a man more money in one night, than the average job paid in a month. About twice a year they would get around to the subject of Ben's uncle. Ben had heard the story many times before, but he still got a special little thrill out of hearing about the time five guys from Lewiston County had cornered his uncle in an old miner's cabin, just over the County line. Old man Brock usually started the tale. "I remember the time when your Uncle Dan and me were running a load of booze up to Lewiston County. Now them boys up there weren't too happy to have us cuttin' in on their territory. In fact, they had already told old Dan what would happen to him if they caught him up there again. But your uncle wasn't the type to worry about small details. We unloaded the booze into the old cabin, and set there waitin' for our contact to come and get it. Seems like we waited fer hours, but I guess it was only forty-five minutes or so. All of a sudden I seen this guy through the window, tryin' to slip up on us in the trees. 'Dan,' I sez, 'we got company.' 'How many?' he sez. I peered through the curtain and watched 'em movin' up. 'Looks like five.' Yer uncle never batted an eye, he just sez, 'hand me that piece of firewood there by the fireplace.' He stood with his back to the wall, right next to the door. Pretty soon I seen the door knob movin'. All of a sudden this big blond headed guy comes bustin' through the door with a gun in his hand. Your uncle swung the firewood right at his face, and knocked him right back out through the door. Another fella ran up fast and met your uncle's fist comin' the other way. Old Dan says, 'try the window', as he slammed the door shut again. I threw a big oak bench through the window and heard somebody screamin' 'my eyes, my eyes.' Then somebody took a shot at the window and the bullet *whined* off the fireplace. Dan sez, 'O.K., we're gonna make a run for it. Get ready. When I open this door, run like hell for the car. If we move fast, they might not get a good shot at us.' 'Hope yer right,' I sez. Pretty soon Dan jerked the door open and yelled NOW. We ran so damn fast, I lost one of my shoes. Yer uncle was out in front of me somewhere and all I could do now was follow the sound of his footsteps crashin' through the woods. I had no idea where the hell I was. After a few minutes I spotted the car. Yer uncle already had it started, and was rolling slowly waitin' fer me to get in. Somebody was awful close, because they were shootin' at us. I dived in through the window and yer uncle *put 'er to the floor*. We bounced down those muddy roads as fast as that Model A could go. We were laughing like hell and trading swigs out of a bottle of corn liquor. 'Hey!' I sez, 'I lost one of my shoes. Yer uncle laughed and sez, 'we AIN'T goin' back for it.' "

Ben Taylor grew up on stories like that about his Uncle Dan. The man had become something of a legend in that county. The other kids at school where Ben attended would often ask questions like "Is Dan Taylor your uncle?" or, "Is it true that your Uncle Dan beat up five guys in Lewiston County?" Ben relished the limelight that his infamous uncle had caused to shine upon him. Moreover, he had a severe case of "hero worship" for his uncle. When they spent time together fishing or hunting, Ben found his uncle to be a man of few words, but a man of definite opinions. The two were very close and Dan taught his nephew the ways of the woods in short, terse sentences. "Don't put your rifle through the fence like that, you'll shoot yourself." "Don't walk along the short grass by the creek, you'll step in a bear trap." Short, to the point and **always** right. Ben never thought about questioning his uncle — what was the point? He'd never told him anything wrong yet . . . except for one time. But Ben wasn't to find out about that for many years to come.

Young Ben did well in school and it soon became evident that his future lie somewhere out there beyond the bounds of Boon County. His Uncle Dan stopped by the house one day to wish him *good luck* on his trip to California. Ben was about to "leave the nest," so to speak, in order to pursue the furtherance of his education at U.C.S.B. in Santa Barbara, California. Somewhere during the course of conversation, on what was to be the last meeting between these two men, Ben mentioned casually that the local insurance man had been after him to get some insurance on his car before he undertook the long drive to Santa Barbara. "Don't like insurance companies," Dan said in his usual word saving style. "They take all your money and then when you need it most, they don't do a goddam thing for you. Save your money and buy somethin' you need with it." Ben let it go at that, but these words were to come back to haunt him some years later.

After completing his education, Ben went on to become a very fine electrical engineer. It wasn't very long before he had acquired all of the trappings of success. He had a beautiful home in Montecito, California, a boat, a porsche and a life style that could only be described as exemplary. The bad news came in 1977. Fires of undetermined origin swept through the beautiful community and exploded homes as if they were giant roman candles. Ben's home at that time had been appraised at upwards of three hundred thousand dollars . . . and not a dime's worth of insurance.

For days afterwards he wandered dazedly through the sickening ruins of his home. After many friends had made indelicate remarks concerning his lack of foresight in failing to insure his property, it began to dawn on him that there was no legitimate, rational reason that he could think of for failing to do so. It all came into focus one evening when he was sitting on the charred steps of what remained of his once beautiful home. His neighbor, Charlie, came wandering over, hands in his pockets, picking his way slowly through the rubble. "Gonna rebuild, Ben?" he asked. "Oh, I don't know," Ben said. "I can't really afford to."

"Well, Ben, when you get your insurance money maybe things will look a little brighter." "Ha, what insurance money?" Charlie looked shocked. "My God man, do you mean to tell me you didn't have **any** insurance on your home?" "I'm afraid not, Charlie." "But, Ben, why?" "Well, my uncle always . . . ." he caught himself, and let the sentence die.

This may come across to you as a rather bizarre example of how a *wrong idea* can surface at a later time in your life to cause you great distress. I want to assure you that the harm done because of erroneous information or "faulty input" by those whom we consider as *unimpeachable sources of learning* is so gigantic in scope, that one thousand books like this one wouldn't even **begin** to scratch the surface of the problem. A great many of the MAJOR problems faced by civilization today are a direct result of *little things* impressed upon *little people* at a time when their attitudes were being formulated.

More about that later, but first let's look closely at Ben Taylor's situation and see if we can discover just exactly what went wrong.

We know that a casual remark made by his uncle was apparently the reason why Ben had developed a dislike for insurance companies. We also know that Ben was of better than average intelligence and therefore should have easily figured out at some point in his life that failing to insure your property in this day and age, is courting disaster.

The unseen ingredient in Ben's attitude was the *immense influence* that his uncle had on him, however casual the remark may have been. You can liken a child, or a young person's mind, to that of a soft, pliable piece of clay. Thoughts are easily implanted, but once the clay hardens, they are difficult indeed to remove. In Ben's case his intelligence and rationale were no match at all for the *bad seed* that had been planted by an uncle whom he admired and loved.

Thanks to federal disaster funds, Ben was later able to rebuild his home. But the financial setback he suffered was of such proportions, that the likelihood of ever recouping his loss is remote, to say the least.

In subsequent years, Ben returned to Boon County on a number of occasions. During one of these visits, he inquired of his mother concerning "Uncle Dan's attitude towards insurance companies." His mother seemed to hesitate slightly and then said, "Why don't you go talk to Mr. Woods, (the local insurance man) and he can tell you all about it."

Later that day, Ben walked into the Woods Insurance office and introduced himself to Mr. Woods. "Ben Taylor, sure I remember you. You're Dan's nephew, how're things in California? Come on in and have a seat."

The two men slid easily into comfortable old chairs, facing each other across Mr. Wood's desk.

"Mr. Woods, I would like to ask you a few questions about my Uncle Dan."

"Sure, Ben, how can I help you?"

"Well, my mother says that Uncle Dan used to carry insurance with you and I'm curious to know what happened. My Uncle Dan seemed to be strongly opposed to insurance, and I'd like to know why."

Mr. Woods replied very calmly, almost respectfully, "Ben, your Uncle and I were once the best of friends. We were both young, back in those days and I think we had a lot of respect for one another. I insured a lot of your Uncle's cars when he was running booze and nobody else would touch him. The problem came after he had wrecked four cars in a row (he held up his fingers to illustrate the point). I tried my damndest to get another company to accept him, but they wouldn't even consider it.

"Your Uncle used to change cars more often than I used to change shirts back in those days. You see, his *profession* at that time required that he take a lot of *unusual* risks. And to put it plainly, he was mad as hell when the insurance company flatly refused to pay the claim when he had his last accident. They sent his insurance payment back to him and wrote him a short letter which basically said, thanks, but no thanks. And Ben, I couldn't honestly blame them."

Ben absorbed the story slowly and then rose from his chair thoughtfully, almost mechanically. "Mr. Woods," he said, "thanks for being honest with me." "You're welcome, Ben, but I want to add one thing. It was *tough* in those days and we all just did the best we could. Your Uncle was a fine man. I watched him support his three sisters and two brothers after your grandfather died from the flu. Some folks might not approve of the way he did things, but I'm gonna tell you straight out. The world could use a few more like Dan Taylor." Ben shook his hand and left the office walking slowly along the river that ran through town, alone except for his thoughts.

So that was it. An *attitude* his uncle had acquired years ago about insurance companies, passed on to him, accepted by him and later on in life returning to cause him great personal loss. "I wonder what Uncle Dan would say about all of this," he thought. But the answer was already in his mind. He knew his uncle would have grieved for years about his loss had he known that it was a direct result of a *casual remark* that Ben had taken very seriously. After all, that was his uncle talking.

Specifically, what is the lesson to be learned from the story of Dan and Ben? There are two actually. ONE—**Let's begin teaching objectivity as a fundamental necessity.** And let's not wait until our youngsters are in college to begin. By that time they have already *accepted* many *false implants* as fact and will undoubtedly be influenced by strong, pre-conceived opinions, prejudices and homespun philosophy. I am NOT, I repeat NOT saying we should abdicate the role of parent-instructor. Quite the contrary. I am urgently suggesting that we can far better fulfill that role by teaching young minds to accept nothing as fact until they have personally investigated on their own and collected the thoughts and viewpoints of many older and more experienced persons. Rather than staunchly following the old tradition of "I said it was this way, now don't argue with me. That's the way it is". Let's instead follow a course which encourages them to ask questions. Only then will they fully appreciate the wisdom of our words and only then shall we stop passing on the sins of the fathers unto the fourth, and fifth generations. What was yesterday's *fact*, is today's *misconception* in many cases. How then can we hope to achieve progress, if we teach our young to accept things as they *appear*, rather than "finding out for themselves"? An attitude that is hampered by *concrete conceptions* is one that has little hope of growing or of *blending* with others.

The other lesson to be learned from Dan and Ben is this: **Let us take great care in the things we represent as fact and let's be vigilant always lest our unguarded statements be accepted as "true" by those whom we love.**

The enormity of impact that unguarded statements can cause are only now beginning to be "fully realized." The world is full of pain as the result of thoughtless parents, friends, business associates, etc. In the course of writing this book, I encountered many scars that time had failed to heal. I marveled at the depth of old wounds and I was moved to sorrow by the countless little hurts that can reach omnipotently out of the past, like an ancient mist, to bring tears to the eyes of the injured heart.

You have also observed the results of these injuries, although you may not have recognized them as such. A case in point. There are literally thousands of people who simply cannot write their names, if someone is watching. Now we're not talking about a few isolated cases here nor are we referring to people with "bad nerves", or some other physical problem. This particular malady is equally distributed throughout the civilized world to both rich and poor, famous and infamous, the successful and the not so successful of people.

It is important to mention that some of these very same people can easily do any other kind of close or skillful task, from threading needles to brain surgery without the slightest hint of any kind of nervousness and they could *care less* who might be watching. The reason? (And this may be hard for you to accept at this point.) When they were very, very young and just beginning to learn how to write their names, a parent, or guardian, or perhaps an older brother or sister, carelessly condemned their little efforts with thoughtless remarks concerning their progress, such as, "Oh Johnny, you'll **never** learn to write your name", or "That looks awful, I can't even read it", or perhaps a double barreled put-down like, "You're so dumb, can't you do anything right?" Needless to say, this kind of encouragement is about as helpful as having your shoelaces tied together. More importantly, the child in question **will accept some of these statements as being true** because of the source and because they are often times too young to have learned the difference between a careless remark and a fact.

Consider the implications: If a small statement can cause someone to have difficulty writing their name in later adult years, how many other terrible things have we done to our loved ones out of ignorance? I can tell you this. Some of the wrongs we perpetrate, remain with our victims for life. I will tell you of two such persons.

Mrs. Flynn

Mrs. Flynn (not her real name) and her husband have been friends of mine for a number of years now. Although they are both considerably older than I, they have that rare quality of being able to put you completely at ease while in their presence. At a recent visit to their home, I gingerly broached the subject of *unhappy memories* of childhood. Mrs. Flynn sat at one side in the room, while Mr. Flynn and I resurrected thoughts from the past of people we had known. I *felt* rather than saw, a slight humorous smile brightening Mrs. Flynn's sun embellished face. She waited patiently, until "Klaus" and I ran out of breath. "I had something like that happen to me long ago," she announced.
Klaus: "Oh, really, honey, what was that?"
Mrs. Flynn: "When I was a young school girl, I used to walk to

school with the same little girlfriend each morning. This went on for a very long time, until one day we had a silly argument about Lord knows what. I remember being extremely upset by the episode and I finally "wound up" the conversation by stating flatly that from now on I would manage to walk to school by myself, thank you! I strode off rapidly in the direction of our one room school house, but as I was putting distance between she and I, I heard her exclaim loudly, 'Yeah, and your butt wiggles when you walk, too.' I never forgot that comment and even up to the present time, I feel very self conscious about my *backsides* whenever there are people watching."
Klaus: "Well, it does wiggle, honey."
Mrs. Flynn: "Oh, shut up!!"
I won't tell you Mrs. Flynn's age, but I will tell you that the incident she spoke of **had** to have occurred well over fifty years ago. Incredible as it may seem, the little comment made by her school chum has been a source of discomfort to her ever since.

Father

My father and I were very close. We had shared abundant laughter together over the years and I miss terribly his great sense of humor and his own special brand of *pungent* wit. Our fishing trips were especially enjoyable to me, because I had him all to myself except for an occasional interruption by some unwary catfish, trout or bluegill that would cause "instant pandemonium" by the mere act of "nibbling" on one of our lines. God, how I miss his laughter!

I used to try everything I could think of to get him started laughing. On one occasion, we were in his rowboat (which he called the Lollypop) about thirty feet from shore. I was sitting in the center of the boat, with my head down trying desperately to thread an uncooperative "night crawler" (worm) onto a sharp hook, which the night crawler had somehow managed to jab into my thumb about six times. Something hit my father's line—hard. He raised his bamboo pole and swung a large fish towards the center of the boat. The fish *flopping all the way* bounced off the top of my head, became unhooked in the meantime and *splashed* into the lake on the other side of the boat. I never even raised my eyes. By this time my father was in stitiches and I was struggling valiantly to keep from cracking a smile. I still hadn't looked at him and somehow this seemed to make it all the more hilarious to him. When he finally managed to catch his breath, I mustered my best "matter of fact" tone and said, "It felt like a flounder, Pop". That started him all over again and the contagious nature of his laughter soon had us both close to tears. Those were the days.

The heart problem was not unknown to the family. I had made several flights back to the midwest during his final years, when close members of the family had called to reluctantly inform me that "he's not going to make it this time". But the great heart kept right on fooling the experts and I learned more about the *true character* of my father in those closing years of his life, than I had even suspected in all of the time that had passed before.

Our last meeting took place in September of 1981. Again I had reacted to the urgent petitions of my mother and other close relatives. "He'll want to see you, please come if you can." Dad had been almost totally blind for about two years. He was not in the hospital this time, but my first glimpse of him sitting in his favorite chair, unable to hear our conversation in the kitchen, told me that his time was very short. I strode to the living room and loudly announced my presence. "Rog.", he said, his strong, dear face beaming, "I kind of figured you'd be showing up." He stood slowly to embrace me strongly, warmly and purposefully rough in a way that only a father and son can understand. I felt the shocking "thinness" of his once powerful frame, and I fought the deep sobs of my soul now assaulting my calm, lighthearted outward guise.

The next several days were great, memorable days. We talked of many things, my father and I. Of dumb things I had done as a boy, of dreams we had dreamed together, of words we had spoken in anger, which we both knew didn't mean a damn thing. It was a time of remembering and a time of "knowing" that we loved each other very much.

On the last evening of my visit, my father began to "drift back" in his memories to a time long ago when he was a lad and when his father (my grandfather) had arrived fresh from Holland to establish a small farm in Minnesota. It was to be a "new beginning" for all of them. The work was hard and the rewards few. Local, long established farmers were not exactly known for their "big hearts" or "helpful attitudes" in those days concerning the new immigrant families in the area and the mere act of "learning to communicate" all over again was a formidable challenge. As was the custom in those days, if you wanted something extra, you worked extra jobs or did extra chores in order to earn the money for it. My father had *something* that he wanted very badly (time had erased the memory of what that *something* was). He struck a bargain with my grandfather whereby the *egg money* would be his at the end of the year, provided my father would work one full year without pay, doing an assortment of heavy duty tasks, like clearing timber from a section of land that was "unfarmable" in its heavily forrested, rock strewn state. I watched my father's face as he spoke, fascinated by the obvious devastation that this "long ago event" had inflicted upon him.

As he told the story, anger and disappointment played darkly across his rugged features. His voice with which he had so often scolded me in strong, vibrant tones, now carried an easily discernable tenor of hurt and betrayal which I could not remember ever having heard before. It seems that after my father had worked very hard for the full year as agreed upon, my grandfather had a change of heart and decided to give the *egg money* to one of my father's sisters instead. For those of you who don't know what *egg money* is, here's a brief explanation. Chickens (of the female persuasion) lay eggs. These eggs are then taken to market and sold to the various grocery stores. The money received for those eggs is—you got it—the egg money.

Getting back to the story. It turns out that my father's sister wanted some new clothes and from all reports that I have been able to gather, she was also my grandfather's favorite. Not a happy situation for my father, but more than that, he had been misled into believing that the money was his for the hard work he had contributed over the previous year. He felt cheated by my grandfather, and the rift that ensued as a result of this incident, eventually caused my father to leave the farm and strike out on his own. To complicate matters, my grandfather died a few years later, leaving *unresolved* the question of honor between the two men. My father ended his story by saying, "Your grandfather told me that a 'Vanderlaan' always keeps his word. Now why would he do such a thing to me?" I made some lame answer about possible pressures or unknown reasons that might later have been explained had grandfather lived. They didn't help. Two months after he had told me this story, my father died. He carried to the end of his life, the scars of an unkept promise, the pain of an unanswered question. Perhaps now, at last,—he understands.

CHAPTER TWO

YOUR VOLATILE ATTITUDE

The teen-age years from thirteen to twenty, insofar as the attitude is concerned, can only be described as *mentally tumultuous*. There is perhaps no other period in the life span during which a human being is subjected to the chaotic perplexities and conflicting loyalties that this season of growth represents. It is a time of clashing perspectives, readjustments, self-awareness, and highly critical self-appraisal. It is the span of time in which you must cast your beliefs and the sum total of your young experience against the hard realities of living.

The first true hints of what your attitude towards life will be begin to manifest themselves at this crossroads in the formulation of your character. Your earlier training, and the *input* you have received up to this crucial point in your life, will now begin to serve you, or unnerve you, whatever the case may be. You will emerge from this time of sorting and testing with most of your "hard rock" attitude established and accepted. Future changes will come slowly and seldom, and then only after some major confrontation of your beliefs causes you to search your soul in an exhaustive effort to arrive at the truth.

I wish with every fiber of my being that high schools and other learning institutions would at this point introduce young minds to an extensive and required course of instruction pertaining to *attitude*, and to the profound and limitless impact that this intangible *ghost of all things believed* will have on their lives.

How terribly archaic, in this age of enlightenment, to allow the young spongelike minds of the nation's pride and joy to embark upon the quest for knowledge, without a thorough understanding of the inherent dangers that abound in permitting others to shape their thoughts *without restrictions*.

We must instill in the world's future generations an insatiable appetite to prove to themselves the validity of all things proposed as knowledge, all things presented as fact. If all opinions, prejudices, viewpoints, theories, and assumptions can be recognized for what they are, we will have indeed taken a monumental step in the right direction. We construct elaborate mechanisms to teach them to absorb — let's teach them to *examine*. We encourage them to accumulate knowledge — let's teach them to *question* knowledge.

There should be a warning label indelibly printed in the minds of all students. "**Caution**, the idea you accept, whether it be from educators, politicians, close family, or your own peers, could be hazardous to your life; **please proceed carefully**." Possibly you've always thought of attitude as "personality" and therefore you may be having some difficulty in justifying (in your own mind) the strong stress I place on *education* as a necessary step in the proper formulation of a healthy attitude. Please bear in mind that the learning process will be the single most important channel through which opinions, beliefs, viewpoints, outlooks, and postures will be established. Attitude is therefore merely a *reflection* of the entire collection.

In no way would I wish to detract from the importance of a pleasant, friendly, outgoing personality as an ingredient of one's attitude. As a matter of fact, we will get into this subject in greater depth at a later point in this book. I do wish to emphasize, however, that attitude encompasses far more than *exterior joviality*, sunny disposition, or a happy-go-lucky outlook on life. The outward shell of an egg, for example, should be clean, bright, and pleasing to the eye if it is to be sold to someone. But these things count for very little aside from appearances. If the ingredients are spoiled, unusable, or unpleasant to the taste, we then have an egg that has no true value, and therefore must be replaced. So it is with many people.

At the present time, attitude is viewed by most institutions of learning as the outward shell of the egg. Very little attention is given to it unless a flaw, or some other unsightly blemish, appears on the surface. Remedial action usually involves a trip to the counselor's office where they attempt to "patch up" the shell of the egg.

If we have here a student who has been occasionally disruptive in class, but is managing somehow to barely "squeek by" with passing grades, a short lecture, it is hoped, will "straighten them out" so that they will once again fit the image of a student. Now if this young person has been influenced by some of his or her peers, to experiment with drugs for example, the path he or she will inexorably follow will lead them to the conclusion that "it's o.k. to fool around with drugs and pot, so long as I make passing grades and stay out of the counselor's office." Such is the rationale that guides many of our young people today during one of the most turbulent periods of their lifetime. I'm sure there's no need for me to spell out the long-term results of this kind of thinking. The "piecemeal, patchwork approach" to the formulation of our young people's attitudes — isn't working.

May I suggest a viable alternative?

Let me state at the outset that I am not an educator. For that reason, I will leave implementation of the details for hands more qualified than my own. Nevertheless, a fresh approach calls for a fresh viewpoint. Here, in my opinion, is the strongest, safest course to follow if we are to have any influence on the attitudes with which our young people will be making decisions during the preparatory period from 13 to 20 years of age.

I would suggest, first of all, a class of instruction entitled:

ATTITUDE

It should commence at the beginning of the freshman year in high school. It should be a **required** course of learning, not an optional one. It should remain somewhat flexible in nature, so that the subject matter could be changed when problems peculiar to a certain area or district must be dealt with. It should be carefully monitored at all times so the participants **and** the instructors never lose sight of its purpose. This will be to enable young people to CONSTRUCT THEIR ATTITUDES IN AN ATMOSPHERE OF TRUTH WHERE ALL AVAILABLE FACTS PERTINENT TO THE SUBJECT WILL BE AIRED OPENLY AND WITHOUT PREJUDICE. It should **never** be allowed to disintegrate into a podium for complaints by the school hierarchy, or even the students for that matter.

The students should be involved in the selection of topics of discussion. This is one way to find out what's on their minds.

The tone of the course, should be established as early as possible, and should follow a format somewhat like the following:

SUBJECT — ATTITUDE
TIME — 9:30
PLACE — THE REC. HALL
ALL THIS WEEK

Orientation on the new ideas and the variety of life styles you will encounter while attending this school.

The danger of accepting new ideas or new habits without learning all of the facts about them. How to "think for yourself" when pressured to join the crowd.

Discussion period, students viewpoints.

Selection of next week's subject matter by the students.

Obviously when one of the students wishes to discuss serious problems, such as drugs and/or marijuana, the instructor must prepare well in advance in order to present the whole story. There is certainly plenty of overwhelming evidence available to illustrate the calamitous results from the prolonged use of any of these substances. Wherever possible, the instructor should bring in persons who have experienced some of the problems associated with these items. Third party influence is certainly far more realistic than the teacher's opinion.

Above all, let it be a class of complete **immunity**, where students may feel free to openly discuss **their** viewpoints without fear of retribution. In an atmosphere of complete frankness, they can **say** the things that they usually only mutter under their breath. The preponderance of facts that will surface on any given subject will cause them to make their own choices in an intelligent, knowledgeable manner, rather than acting as the result of "peer pressure" or ignorance.

I feel very strongly that a class such as the one I have just described, should be an ongoing part of the teenager's education in order to be truly effective. My reasons for this are plentiful. First of all, let's identify some of the trouble spots. *Unfavorable peer pressure* is pretty well recognized as a source of serious difficulties for a great many students. Why? The answer is fairly obvious —**because it's constant**. Before school begins, during the school day, and after school lets out, peer pressure remains in effect. Now how can we hope to combat an influence of that magnitude without maintaining a forum for the exploration of truth and the dissemination of facts for at least a portion of the time that they're in school? Secondly, one of the strongest drives evident in the makeup of the average young student is *the desire to belong*. This need is so powerful in many young people that it regularly becomes the source of the first real problems between parent and child. It comes in many disguises and often goes unrecognized, but it is there. Should the "nice" boy or girl suddenly become involved in drugs, or some other illegal activity, without explanation; you can just about bet your bottom dollar that *the need to belong* to some group, or some collection of friends, is at the root cause of the problem.

I maintain that the most effective means of dealing with the destructive nature of such groups of people is to **haul out their**

actions for all to see in an open atmosphere of inquiry. The assembly of questions and the examination of possible consequences and probable long-term results, will ultimately prove the perpetrators of these acts to be either terribly misled, or plain stupid. More importantly, those who observe these discussions will easily be able to assemble the facts for themselves and to draw their own conclusions as to the wisdom of their actions.

If there is a problem of theft in the school or in the area, get a reformed convict to present his story to the class. If there is a drinking problem, ask for a speaker from A.A.; they'll be glad to help. It is a thousand times more effective to listen to those who have suffered as the result of their respective follies, than to look at all the charts, all the pictures, and all of the warnings in the world.

To those of you who are involved in education, if the title "attitude" seems to sound a little too intimidating for a course of study, then call your class *truth forum*, *sound off*, *students inquiry*, or whatever. But **do** establish a platform from which you can counter the *negative inputs* that threaten to steal the fine minds you have worked so hard to improve.

In addition to the "well known" destructive habits that frequent our schools, such as liquor, drugs, pot, smoking, etc., there is a formidable array of lesser known attitude problems. I believe they should be dealt with from the very same platform of truth, bearing in mind at all times that its purpose is to *"head off"* incorrect formulation of attitudes **before** they become hard and fast implants. Let's take a hypothetical example, and perhaps I can more clearly establish the procedure that I believe should be followed in order to accomplish the desired results.

Bob Coleman is a student at "your school high". Yesterday he became angry at the track coach, and wound up tearing two of the soap dispensers off the wall, above the sinks in the men's room. Mr. Fisher is the moderator for this month's attitude class. He begins today's session by describing in detail the events that led up to, and the destruction that followed in the wake of this angry outburst. The act of destruction itself comes across as rather "bizarre conduct" in the cold, passionless light of a new day. Mr. Fisher continues.

Mr. Fisher: Now Bob, would you please tell us what your feelings were when you tore the soap dispensers off the wall? I mean did it make you feel better, did your anger diminish, or did you stay mad after you did it?

Bob: I don't know, I just got mad.

Mr. Fisher: Yes, I know you were mad, but stop and think for a minute. Did the act itself help you in any way?

Bob: (After a moment's silence) Well . . . No, I didn't feel any better.

Mr. Fisher: Did it somehow make you feel like you were "getting even" with Coach Hobbs?

Bob: Oh, no, I wasn't trying to get even — I was just mad.

Mr. Fisher: Well would you say that tearing up something is the thing to do when you get mad?

Bob: Well . . . No, I guess not.

Mr. Fisher: O.K., so you don't recommend tearing up property when you get mad. Now one more thing, Bob, who do you think should pay for the damages?

Bob: Well it's school property — no big deal.

Mr. Fisher: I'm sorry but it **is** a big deal; someone has to pay for the damages. This school is supported by the taxes paid by the parents of each of these students. Now do you think we should have each of their parents chip in to pay for your anger, or shall we just send a bill to **your** parents?

Bob: . . . Well, I'm the one who did it, so I'll pay for the damages.

Mr. Fisher: Did you hear that class? Bob says he did it so he will pay for the damages. I think that's exactly the right attitude. Bob, stop by after class and we'll work out a payment plan for you.

(Mr. Fisher continues, but he is no longer directing his remarks to Bob specifically.)

I think we've learned something from Bob today, but let's carry it on a little farther. Does anyone present think that they are justified in breaking something when they get angry? Let me see the hands.

Karen: Mr. Fisher, I really don't see any harm in breaking a pencil, or in throwing something once in awhile if it helps to relieve the tension.

Mr. Fisher: The problem, Karen, is not in the small, unimportant things that you might break today, but rather in the *attitude-habits* that you will form as you go through life by satisfying anger with an act of destruction. As your problems get larger, your acts of violence will also increase.

Who can say where you will draw the line? Will you find yourself beating your children when they misbehave? Will you wreck your husband's car when you have a serious quarrel? Will your anger demand someday that the only act that will satisfy your terrible rage is to **kill** someone who has wronged you? No, destruction is **not** the way to deal with anger. I'm sure Bob had no intention of tearing up school property yesterday, but rage has a way of overwhelming one's power of reason when allowed to go unchecked. Now who in this class has seen examples of uncontrollable tempers?

By his system of probing and answering, Mr. Fisher was able to solicit many stories of runaway tempers, and of the unpleasant results that ensued. This participation by the class, made the lesson far more memorable, and illustrated the reality of the problem in a manner far superior to a two hour lecture on good conduct, for example.

Yes, I know there are those who will say that the concept of putting the offender "on the spot", so to speak, is cruel, and may somehow damage them psychologically. I disagree absolutely. Let them learn **NOW** that there is a price to be paid for stupid conduct. But let them learn it in a constructive, analytical fashion so that they may *understand* the lesson. The specter of having to "face up" to one's peers, and of having their acts "spread out in front of God and everybody" is a far greater deterrent than a friendly little chat with a counselor.

What this system says is . . . Here's the guy who did it. What did he accomplish by doing this? Was it smart or dumb and what's going to happen if he keeps on doing it?

That pretty well covers the subject.

As The Twig Inclines

The high school, young adult experience is fraught with surprises for parents, and other interested observers. Character changes, and sometimes complete *attitude reversals*, can, and often times, do occur as young people wade through the onslaught of countless winds of doctrine both social and academic.

Children who had always exhibited an inclination towards courage and strength can suddenly become strangely shy and fearful. The reverse is also true. Those who had always been inclined to "take a back seat" in the competitive arena of early childhood may somehow "find themselves" in the mixed conglomeration of vociferous clamorings for their attention.

Anyone who has observed the conduct of these young people over a fairly long period of time will readily agree that the person who emerges out of this experience will be for the most part, the finished product, minus certain shades of polish which they will accumulate further on down the road. The "refining process", of course, is an ongoing thing that will hopefully be an integral part of their makeup for the rest of their lives.

This is also the interval during which their contemporaries begin to hang short, descriptive labels on them. In almost all cases the labels are no more than *mini-descriptions* of their attitudes. For example: "She's a good student, but she's such a sourpuss." or "I like her, but she's so selfish." or "Jim's a real 'hunk', but he's so dense." For the first time in their lives they are beginning to "classify" and "type" one another as the elements of their respective attitudes surface through the veneer of their outward appearances.

What a troublesome time it is for some. How often have you heard remarks like, "I wouldn't want to be sixteen again for anything" or the all too familiar, "I wish I knew then, what I know now." We tend to forget, as time goes by, that growing up was far from being a picnic. Adolescence, let's face it, is not all that it's cracked up to be. We should try to remember that as our children pass through this stressful time.

The social functions that occur as a normal happenstance of the *"learnin' and yearnin'"* period are great arenas of attitude exposure and projection. The quiet observer at a school dance, for example, (if you can find a way to remain a quiet observer while at a school dance) will most certainly be able to read *attitude signs* all over the place.

Beautiful, blonde headed Karon will be laughing loudly with her girl friends, all the while glancing casually around the room in order to see who is watching. Some of the less popular girls will be grouped elsewhere, enjoying the security of an unspoken alliance, formed at some earlier time, for the purpose of protecting each of them from the terrible specter of being alone. Still others will be by themselves, sitting stoop shouldered, wearing a fixed smile, and radiating louder than words, all of the tell-tale signs that say "I don't expect to be asked to dance this evening; I only came because I like the taste of punch."

There is another who will be sitting alone, but this young lady will be dressed in the regal garb of *confidence*. Her manner will state loudly and unmistakably that she needs no other upon whom to lean. She will be sitting tall and straight, and her smile will shine generously and without prejudice upon the popular and the unpopular. She will be relaxed and sure of herself. Those who approach her will do so respectfully, without fear, knowing full well that in no way will they be rebuffed or belittled. There will be no subtle shading of the voice, or cooling of the smile to indicate displeasure. Favored indeed is the young person who has been thus blessed, at so early an age, with the rich gift of *compassion*.

The boys will also be showing their wares, parading before all onlookers the outward signs and actions which proclaim their attitudes in clear, concise terms, allowing little room for misinterpretation. Johnny Blake will be, not so secretly, spiking the punch and staggering slightly whenever others are watching. He will be speaking with a noticeable slur, and verifying once again that he has no regard for protocol or anything else, save the great need he has to be recognized. Bill Brown will demonstrate his firm belief in physical strength by dancing with two girls at the same time by lifting them off their feet and carrying them around the dance floor. Before the night is over he will be fighting, or arguing loudly with some poor guy who can't understand what has happened. Jeff Hunt will be politely asking the girls to dance, and then smoothly and expertly putting on a show for the unlucky ones who have to sit this one out. His manner says, "I'm Jeff Hunt; I'm a good dancer and quite a guy, but if you play your cards right maybe . . . just maybe I will ask you to dance. No lack of self-confidence there.

The show goes on, and during the course of the evening you will be able to see the full gamut of *acquired attitudes* demonstrated for you. You will see cruelty, compassion, concern, rudeness, fairplay, tenderness, mischief, humor, and all of the other telltale signs which indicate what the person you are watching is really like.

Astonishing as it may seem, a perfect stranger could walk into the room, and in a very short time this person could tell you with surprising accuracy what each of the people you are observing is like. You see, the *attitude* has now begun to control the *action*, and from approximately this stage in life the attitude will begin to broadcast to others what they are.

In my book, *Persuasion* (El Camino Publishers, 1981), I mentioned that when you first meet someone, you have approximately twenty seconds during which that person will make up their mind whether they like you or not. Maybe not consciously, but they **will** decide on the spot, and that decision will stick ninety-five per cent of the time. Now, should they decide that they don't like you, it is very definitely an uphill battle to change their mind.

What's the reason for this? The answer is surprising. People learn as they go through life to rely upon their *attitude-readings* and **rarely** do they mistrust this information. Experience has taught them to "pick up" certain little attitude signs. Nothing dramatic, it's more of a feeling. But your attitude speaks volumes about who, and what you are to the *instincts* of those whom you are meeting for the first time.

Be careful how you allow your *attitude* to form. You will have to live with it for the rest of your life.

CHAPTER THREE
INSTANT ATTITUDE READINGS

We know that there is a certain "something" that others can pick up concerning our attitudes. And we know that it reveals its presence primarily to the *"instinct"* of others as mentioned in the last chapter. But just for the fun of it, let's talk about some of the more obvious ways that we can learn to evaluate the attitudes of people that we feel obliged to come in contact with. I have chosen this particular spot in the book to examine at length some of these *"glaring"* attitude traits because the normal course of events that most of us have followed, and that some of us have yet to follow, will lead directly from high school to a job, or on to expand your knowledge in college, or a trade school of your choice. In any case, this will mean that you will be mixing with people whom you have never met before, and therefore you will have to trust to your ability to judge the character of others, or learn to do *instant attitude readings.*

Perhaps you have never really thought about it before, but the skill you can develop in reading the attitudes of others is no different than any other skill you might wish to learn, in that it requires *concentration* and a reasonable amount of *dedication* if you truly want to derive some benefit from the new thoughts you will be exposed to. My father used to be fond of saying "education is expensive, even for dummies." What he was implying, of course, was the universally known fact that if you're not willing to learn from the mistakes and misfortunes of others, you will most certainly learn the hard way by making them all yourself.

As elementary as some of these observations will seem to some, I would nevertheless beg your indulgence, in deference to the younger people who may possibly profit from some of the thoughts we will share in this chapter. Most of us who have been through the school of hard knocks can easily think of a time when we "wished someone had warned us" about people like "you know who." Once out of the comfortable circle of friends we have known for years, we seem to pass through a period of time during which we encounter every kind of "screwball" imaginable. Most are really harmless, others are to be pitied, and some are dangerous. Youth has a way of "diving in" to most unhappy situations with little or no regard for the *"attitude signs"* that are there to read for those who prefer to "look, before they leap." By way of illustration, I would like to again have you imagine a hypothetical situation with me. Let's take a problem that is faced by many young people at some point in their life, and see if we can implement some *"instant attitude readings"* into the picture. Once the procedure is clear, it will not be difficult to visualize the possible advantages that this approach has to offer.

Sandra

Sandra Stoneman is a young lady who has had the good fortune of being born to upper middle class parents with a solid background and an unwavering dedication to the pursuit of knowledge. It should be noted that Sandra does not always agree with the rigid self-discipline that both her father and mother seem to have mastered over the years. Leaving home to attend college in a distant city was an experience of conflicting emotions for Sandra. On the one hand she was glad to be "on her own at last", but at the same time there had been this strong tugging at her heart as the plane began moving away from the terminal and her parents had seemed to shrink in size while the powerful thrust of the engines roared a defiant farewell. This was not the way she would have liked it. There were so many things she wished she had said, and yet their last few moments had been filled with idle chatter concerning insignificant little details. Did you pack that large tube of toothpaste? (Yes, Mom.) I hope you brought something to change into when you get there? (I did Mom.) Now don't forget to call us the minute you get there. (I will Mom, I promise.) And then there was Dad. He said very little aside from an occasional "You be careful honey" or "If there's anything you need, you call now." But he had this strained, almost angry, look on his face, and Sandra had known from all the years past that her Daddy was "dealing with" his sadness.

As she peered out of the plane window, she had seen them both standing there: Dad with his arm around Mom's shoulder, Mom dabbing at her eyes with a white handkerchief. Sandra had tried to appear "the sophisticated, world traveler" for the benefit of anyone who might be watching, but her heart had whispered a gentle "good-bye Mom and Dad" as she fought the great lump that had forced its way into her throat.

Now at last the "hubbub" of getting a place to "settle in" for the school semester was behind her; all that remained to be done was the selection of a roommate who would share the expenses of her small apartment. "Dad would be proud of me", she thought. She had placed a small ad in the local paper, and today she would be interviewing those students who had replied and who, like herself, were tryng to get by as inexpensively as possible.

(Note)

For the sake of simplicity, we are going to assume that Sandra has been thoroughly briefed on *"Instant attitude readings"* by her Father, and that she will be practicing this technique as she interviews her callers for the purpose of selecting a roommate. Now back to Sandra's story.

In keeping with her Father's instructions, Sandra had made a short check list for the purpose of evaluating the various *"attitude signs"* exhibited by her callers. She had a place for their name, address, and phone number. This was followed by a chart where she could indicate "good" or "bad" with a simple checkmark at the end of singly descriptive words such as — neatness, thoughtfulness, disposition, personal appearance, general attitude (negative, or positive), concern for other people's property, honesty, feelings about school, and so on.

She now sat thoughtfully by her front window, briefly reviewing her notes, as she awaited the arrival of her first prospective "roomy". Estelle Phillips was scheduled to arrive at 10:00 A.M. It was now 10:20 and, as yet, there was no sign of Estelle. Sandra let another ten minutes tick by and then made a short notation on her chart. It read, "Late, no phone call". Another fifteen minutes dragged by before Sandra's thoughts were ruthlessly torn from her by the protesting squeel of tires up at the corner, a half block from her apartment. A late model car crunched to a stop against the curbing in front of the apartment a few seconds later.

An attractive young lady sprang from the side opposite the driver, followed by the unwinding of a tall young man on the driver's side. They slammed their doors, and cut across the new grass bounding up the several steps to the front door. Sandra rose to meet the insistant pounding on her front door.

"Hi!! Are you Sandra Stoneman?" the young lady beamed.

"Yes I am," Sandra replied.

"Hey, I'm sorry I'm late. My boyfriend had to pick up some cigarettes, and we 'almost' got lost trying to find you." (A pretty difficult thing to do in the small college town).

"Please come in," Sandra said. "Have a seat so we can talk."

"Thank you very much," the young lady gushed. "Oh I **like** the apartment; you have it fixed up so cute."

"Thanks," Sandra Said. "It's 'getting there' little by little."

The next few minutes were an exercise in meaningless chatter. The conversation went something like this:

"Will you be staying for a full four years?" Sandra queried.

"Oh I don't know. It depends on Jimmie," she grinned as she shot her boyfriend a meaningful glance.

(So that's his name, Sandra thought.) "Yes, but I would like to know how long you would be sharing expenses on the apartment."

"Oh I'll probably be here for quite a while; those little kitties on the fireplace are so cute. Jimmie, don't you think those kitties are cute?"

"Uh huh."

"Would you be able to afford $150 per month rent?"

"That's a little high, but maybe I could make it; say could I use your hair brush for a second? I left mine in the car."

Sandra was momentarily shocked, "Uh, I'm sorry I don't loan my hair brush out."

(Jimmie decided to get his two cents in.) "Roommates have to share a lot of things you know," he said in his deepest "macho" tone.

"Not my hairbrush," Sandra replied lightly.

"Can I use your bathroom?" the young lady asked.

"Sure, it's right back there." As she headed for the bathroom, Sandra noticed that she flicked her cigarette ashes on the hall carpet while enroute.

Jimmie speaketh. "How about the water and gas? Who pays for those?"

"Well I'm sure we can work out something fair — if Estelle and I decide to live here together."

"It's best to put those things in writing," Jimmie said.

Sandra was grinning pleasantly, but she was thinking to

herself, "I wonder what this creep would do if I went to the fireplace, grabbed the two little plaster kitties, and pounded numerous and sundry lumps on his stupid head."

Fortunately, Estelle returned in the nick of time. "I just love the apartment," she said. "The blue toilet is really neat."

"I didn't hear it flush," Sandra was thinking.

Jimmie decided to venture one more "pearl of wisdom" before departing. "If you decide to move in here, Estelle, I had better not hear about you girls having a bunch of damn parties for your school chums."

Sandra felt a growing impatience with these two thoughtless people; she stood abruptly, and started "herding" them nonchalantly towards the front door. "Thank you for stopping," she said. "I have others to interview, and I will make a decision by the end of the week. Estelle, I'll give you a call Saturday if you like".

"O.K. But don't call before ten. Jimmie likes to sleep in on the weekends."

She answered with a pleasant "all right," but in her secret mind she was thinking, "Sweetie Pie, your boyfriend's brain has been 'sleeping in' for life."

After they left—again across the new grass, Sandra sat down to think about the experience, and to make a great many check marks in her little chart. My God, she thought, is this what I'm going to have to settle for? How right my Father was when he said, "Sandra, the world is full of — screwballs. You haven't learned that yet, but you will — you will."

She questioned her own fairness. Maybe I'm being too critical. After Dad's lecture, I began looking for *attitude signs*. Well I sure found them. No, Dad was right. Better to find out now, than after they move in.

Her thoughts were interrupted by a knocking at the door. She was surprised to find a nice looking young man about her own age gazing down into her eyes. "Are you Sandra Stoneman?" he said.

"Why — Yes I am," she answered.

"I understand you're looking for a roommate."

She chose her words carefully, "I have a number of people to interview before making a decision. Why?"

"Well I'm Randy Fisher. May I come in?"

"Uh—I suppose so; how can I help you?"

He entered casually, confidently, and started the conversation in a very matter-of-fact tone. "I'm going to be attending college here for another three years, and I'm looking for a place to stay. I have a good part-time job and money is no problem. Your location here is ideal for my purposes. It's close to school, as well as my job."

"Now wait a minute," she said. "I'm looking for a **female** roommate; I am **not** looking for a man."

"Why not? You're here to learn aren't you? Half of the girls in college are living with a man."

"That's their business, but it is **not** the way I choose to do things."

"Come on lady, you're not all that pure, unless you've been living in a cave."

"Good-by Mr. Fisher."

"What's the big deal? Everybody's doing it."

"I—am not."

"Hey, you don't know what you're missing."

"I'll chance it."

"The last girl I lived with paid all of the rent for me, and begged me not to leave her."

"Good-bye, Mr. Fisher."

"I can make you feel real good, Sandra — real good."

"Get out!!"

"You don't really mean that."

"Get out you creep, or I'll scream bloody murder."

"O.K. — O.K. Don't get excited." He stood, and walked slowly towards the door. "If you change your mind, you can find me at the gas station up the street."

She didn't answer, but her glare followed him out the door. "I can't believe this," she was thinking, "I ran a simple little ad in the paper, and it's turned out to be an open invitation to Looney Tunes. Isn't there somebody out there who wants to get an education? Who just wants a decent place to live for the next few years?"

The days that followed went swiftly that week. She had decided to postpone her interviews until the weekend, when she knew the owner would be in the next apartment. Unhappily, the weekend was upon her before she knew it. Reluctantly, she agreed to see one "Cathy Landis" just after lunch on Saturday. Promptly at 1 o'clock there was a firm rapping at the front door. Sandra braced herself, ready for anything from "Dracula" to the "wicked old witch" of the west. As she strode purposefully towards the door, she made herself a mental promise. "If that's another 'scuzz bucket,' this will be the shortest interview in history."

What she saw pleased her. Cathy Landis was neatly dressed in a pretty blue dress with white polka dots and a white collar and trim. She looked, at once, both cool and lively. She had a large, red belt at her slim waist, and her dancing brown eyes promised both honesty and mischief.

Sandra liked her at once, and began giving her good checkmarks on her mind's appraisal chart. What was it her father used to say? "If you allow youself to *'feel'* another person's attitude, your judgement will rarely be wrong." She found that she did not want to be wrong about Cathy Landis. Nevertheless, she determined to make a proper interview out of this meeting, rather than running the risk of sharing the apartment with somebody straight out of "Cooksville."

Pleasantly, the two girls chatted on about their similar backgrounds, about their goals while in College, and then, inevitably, about their boy friends. Sandra found it difficult to "ride herd" on the conversation. They were like long lost friends who hadn't seen each other in a long time. In addition to that, Sandra had the distinct impression that with Cathy — what you see is what you get. They slid into the subjects of rent, what each expected from the other in this "partnership," what the rules would be on boys, and how they would share in the chores, with the greatest of ease. Sandra *"felt"* her young friend's frankness, and one by one she penciled in the favorable checkmarks that collectively assembled the portrait of a warm and compassionate roommate and friend.

Cathy moved in on the following Saturday. The *"attitude readings"* that Sandra had put to use in the selection of a roommate proved to be both accurate, and beneficial. How much more sensible this approach had been, as opposed to just grabbing the first person who showed up at the door and hoping that things would work out. The forethought that Sandra had employed in the utilization of *"attitude readings"* may spare her "God knows what" in the next few years. How unfortunate that many persons prefer to "act in haste" and gamble on the outcome.

Ivan Is Watching

The Ivan I refer to in this case is not the great Russian bear, but rather the "big brothers of business" who must judge a man's attitude very carefully before entrusting to him the awesome power that comes with decision making at the higher levels. Say what you will about the corporate structure of the nation, but give credit where credit is due. The men who control the gargantuan industrial complexes of this, or any other nation, do so with full knowledge of the incalculable risk involved in placing power, or purse strings, into the hands of those persons whom they do not know absolutely — *by attitude*.

Meetings, dinners, get togethers, parties, and home visits are all calculated to enable the grand masters of leadership to constantly monitor the pulse, and even the heartbeat, of *"attitude" trends."* Mistaken attitude readings can be, and often are, financially fatal. So the concept of *"instant attitude readings"* is by no means a new practice. It is my belief, however, that until we begin to **teach** attitude, the possibility of miscalculation will remain far too great to be acceptable. History has taught us repeatedly that many men who have ridden to power on the coattails of personality, popular causes, or the ability to relate to the masses, have done so without once being stopped along the way to have their *"attitude"* questioned. We later have learned, much to our chagrin, that the true attitude of that person was that of a despot or a dictator, totally lacking in conscience or compassion. The world has suffered greatly as the result of this brand of apathetic oversight. We tend to generalize too much. We define attitudes with short, comfortable descriptions. He's "happy-go-lucky" or "irresponsible" or "stubborn" or "determined" or "friendly" or "temperamental." This need that we seem to have for brevity leaves a lot to be desired, if we are to place any confidence in descriptions.

It is, nevertheless true, that the *business world* does practice *"instant attitude readings"* beginning at some of the lowest levels of employment. They may not refer to them as such, but there are a vast number of job applications specifically designed to draw a miniature picture of the applicant. Interspersed with the questions concerning ability, experience, aptitude and other desirable qualifications, you will find little semi-silly, innocent looking probes. The answers you give, and the **manner** in which you reply will be carefully scrutinized for some hint as to the nature of your Attitude. You will see questions like "What do these four birds have in common?" — "Which is your favorite sport?" — "Why did you leave your last job?" — "Would you be willing to work Sundays?" — "Would you mind cutting your hair if asked to do so?", etc.

Admittedly, they are crude at best, and a valid argument could be made as to their worth. Surprisingly though, they do occasionally smoke out some of the more radical elements. On the other side of the coin, however, there are probably just as many persons unjustly classified by this Neanderthal technique. Our society is still dealing with the bits and pieces of *"personality"* when, in fact, we should be training and defining the "whole" of the attitude. It's a lot like trying to treat poison ivy—one blister at a time.

The most common form of *"instant attitude readings"*, as practiced by employers, is still "the job interview" or "a talk with the boss." This ancient, and respected, ritual is still one of the best. It is, in my opinion, far superior to any form of written examination. The attitude signs are there to be seen by the experienced eye, and the *"unseen"* factors which we don't really understand as yet will somehow make their presence known as surely as though they were chiseled in marble. The Boss who has done many interviews over the years will have developed a strong sensitivity to the *"unspoken"* "attitude signs." The "overall" complexion of the attitude will "drift" from the conversation like a pleasant perfume, or perhaps like an unpleasant odor. But it will be recognizable.

The more obvious *"attitude signs"* will speak loudly and clearly. If a young man, for example, shows up 20 minutes late for a job interview, that's strike one. If he slouches in the chair with his hands in his pockets, that's strike two. If his shoe laces are untied and he "lights up" and drops the ashes in his pants cuff, that's strike three, and he's out. The outward *attitude signs* say volumes about an individual, and they are easy to read. If a young person "charges" through a restaurant door and lets it swing back without regard for the little old lady behind him, he has no concern for others. If the gas station attendant meanders slowly out to your car and says, "Yeah?" then he is not courteous. If he pumps the gas and takes your money without offering to check your oil or wipe your windshield, then he's also lazy. If your neighbor walks his dog in the mornings and lets him "do his thing" on your lawn, he has no regard for other people's property and none for you. If the waitress at your local restaurant slaps your coffee down, slopping it over the side in the process, then burns your toast and serves it with a straight face, you probably eat at the same place I do.

Attitude signs are everywhere and are easy to read. Learn to look for them, especially where it involves business, or a relationship that can affect you. It doesn't take an Einstein to realize that you wouldn't go into business with someone who steals candy bars from the grocery store.

The same is true in affairs of the heart. If you get involved with someone who treats their parents and their brothers and sisters like dirt, don't think that you're going to reform them. Get out of the relationship before you become another victim.

The **bright** side of *"instant attitude readings"* is the joy you will experience in being able to "spot" the good and decent qualities which prevail in the vast majority of the world's peoples. How refreshing to the soul it is to witness a young man or woman in the act of showing a kindness to an elderly person. Whenever I see an act of compassion such as that, I silently whisper a compliment to the parents. "God bless you, 'Mother,' wherever you are. You did a great job with the kids."

We are admonished in the Bible not to cast our pearls before swine. I believe that lesson was meant to be taken in its broadest sense, and not only as it pertains to religion. The loftier qualities of the human spirit were intended to be shared with those who can appreciate them. They were not meant to be squandered on the thoughtless, the heartless, or those who are so totally involved in "self" that they have no room left for anyone else.

What a tragic waste to see a young person, with their whole life before them, living precipitously on the edge of destruction in the mistaken belief that they can "change" someone who is devoid of tenderness. Like a mighty whirlpool, they are drawn in and their own lives are shattered, often beyond repair, as the brutality of such an alliance snuffs out the flame of hope, and crushes the tender petals of love, like the flower of a nation beneath an invader's boots. Learn, instead, to *"read"* the attitude, and then to respect and give credence to whatever your "reading" tells you. Acts of kindness, consideration, fondness, tenderness, compassion, selflessness, generosity, concern, pity, and modesty are everywhere. Look for the bearers of those qualities. These are the people with whom you should share your time — and even your life.

Before we leave the subject of "instant attitude readings," let's play a little game, and perhaps I can encourage you to start practicing this art on your own. Imagine, if you will, that you and I are having lunch together. We are sitting in a medium priced restaurant, and we are about to begin practicing *"instant attitude readings."* You have a pad and pencil with you, and as I describe the people who come through the door, you will write down your impression of their attitudes or any "feeling" you get about them based upon my descriptions. Are you ready? O.K., here we go.

The first gentleman who enters is dressed in a red plaid jacket. He has a grey cap on, similar to the ones they used to wear in the thirties. He avoids people by going to the far end of the dining room and taking a seat by the window. He doesn't look around, but goes straight to the menu and after scanning it very briefly, sits patiently waiting for the waitress to come. He has heavy work shoes on, and his trousers are worn. His cap has a couple of silver badges pinned on it. He keeps glancing out the window as though he is expecting someone.

Try to describe his occupation, and more importantly, see if you can "pick up" something about his attitude from this description.

The next gentleman to enter is dressed in a business suit. He is holding a brown paper bag which he carries to a far table. Upon seating himself, he removes a sandwich from the bag and starts yelling for the waitress to bring him some coffee. He has two refills, and when he leaves he does not tip the waitress, although we can see through the window that he drives off in a late model car. His shoes were expensive looking, and he had a large diamond ring on his left hand.

What's your impression of this guy??

Our last customer enters wearing cowboy boots and the standard western attire. He sits at the bar, tilts his hat back on his head, and although the bartender is close by, he tells one of the waitresses to "Bring me a Bud, will you honey?" While he is sitting there (four beers) the phone rings for him twice. The conversations are fairly long, and he seems to be argueing with someone. When he leaves, he doesn't pay for the beers, but yells at the bartender as he goes out the door, "Catch you Friday." He also fails to leave a tip.

How about this one? Is he a big spender with a bar tab and lots of business calls? Or is he a harried husband who should have been home some time ago?

I'll let you make your own guesses. It is true that there could be several explanations for each of their actions, but if you will listen to your "instincts" you will be correct.

The point is, we look, but we do not see. The evidence is all around us, but we ignore it and listen instead to whatever we are being told.

By the way, I enjoyed having lunch with you. I'm a little short today would you mind picking up the check? I'll catch you the next time. (Sound familiar?)

The focal point which should be your "guiding light" when doing "instant attitude readings" is — love.

Those who are the possessors of this "greatest of all" gifts are all about you. The ability to love cannot be concealed. It "spills over" into the everyday activities of the people in whom it lives and grows. It can be seen in the sympathetic, gentle concern shown to a small child, in the misty eye which beholds the grandeur of a lovely sunset. In the unspeakable wonder which glows from the face of a loving person as they absorb the strains of a beautiful melody. The heart that loves, is in awe of the beauty that can be seen all around us. It feels humble beside the majesty of the great forests. It gazes with respect, and a peaceful swelling of its innermost self, at the "hand painted" magnificence of the massive, towering mountain ranges. It recognizes, and acknowledges, the unmistakable signature of the "master designer" of all good things, great and small. And from this source it renews and refreshes itself for the purpose of abundantly sharing, without restraint, the priceless, indescribable wellspring of life — the gift of love.

The attitude which suffers the most, the one which projects its bitterness in the hardness of facial features as well as the callous disregard for the sensitivities of others, is the attitude that is lacking in this most important of all ingredients. Profound in meaning as this statement may be, I will state without qualification that "the greater the ability to love, the greater the attitude." The greater the **lack** of ability to love, the poorer the attitude is likely to be.

And so it is that all of the great teachers, both past and present, be they men of religion, men of learning, philosophers, playwrites, authors, philanthropists, or seekers of truth in any other walk of life, continually strive to unveil for us the essence of being. The message at the heart of their dispensations remains unchanged. Love is the answer. And the lack of it, is at the root cause of most of the world's ills.

ATTITUDE

If I speak in the tongues of men and of angels, but have not love, I am a noisy gong or a clanging cymbal. And if I have prophetic powers, and understand all mysteries and all knowledge, and if I have all faith, so as to remove mountains, but have not love, I am nothing. If I give away all I have, and if I deliver my body to be burned, but have not love, I gain nothing. (1st. Corinthians 13.—1st. through 3rd. verse)

The Holy Bible

On a recent occasion, I received a phone call from a friend inviting me to join him for lunch. I suggested that we meet at a restaurant which overlooks the harbor in Santa Barbara. He agreed, and soon we were walking up the steps together, anticipating a leisurely lunch on the outdoor terrace which affords a spectacular view of not only the boat harbor but the distant mountains as well.

As the young waitress seated us at our table, I felt a tinge of elation as I drank in the beauty that was surrounding us. My friend was preoccupied with "trouble at the office." He led off the conversation with a vivid description of "life in the fast lane" as practiced by some of his employees. I listened politely, trying hard not to appear bored; although, I must admit that I had some difficulty in concentrating on this tale of woe while the whole world around me was bursting with vibrant life. I must tell you that we are close friends, and that I would enjoy his company regardless of what kind of mood he was in, and I feel certain that he would "put up" with **my** "bellyaching" if the situation were reversed. I do often feel, however, that Frank (not his real name) has allowed himself to become a victim of *"purpose-blindness."* He is often so thoroughly involved in the "nuts and bolts" of putting his dream together that he loses sight of the reasons for which he began his dream in the first place. As we ate our lunch, his story took on the complexion of a damn good soap opera. The characters involved slowly emerged from his colorful descriptions. Every so often I would throw in an intelligent reply like — Uh huh — really? — You're kidding, etc. This seemed to be sufficient reaction for Frank though. He continued to unfold the strange saga of who did what to whom, why a certain secretary always has blood shot eyes, and why the new kid in shipping just can't seem to make it to work on time. My friend could be so brutally honest in his storytelling, that he made me feel somewhat like a peeping Tom. I kept waiting for the commercial — it never came. I did manage to slip in a couple of quickies when I caught him with his mouth full, though.

Throughout this rather one-sided exchange, I glanced casually about the harbor. It was teaming with drama — real drama. I watched an aged fisherman sitting in the familiar comfort of his boat, tending his nets in the warmth of the sun. I wondered about his life. Perhaps he could tell us stories of "giant" fish who had destroyed his nets, or of strange shores where strange and wonderful people had saved him from his leaky old boat. I watched with admiration as a large, graceful seagull embraced the soft, flirtatious breezes. I smelled the fresh salty air, and heard the deep, throaty bubbling of a diesel boat engine in the distance. The harbor was filled with sails of all sizes. The vivid "blues" and "whites" and "reds" rocked easily in the gentle waters as if to say, "we are here, aren't we gorgeous?" Even the rhythmic squeeking and groaning of the boats at anchor had found a melody they could sing in harmony with the placid "splosh", "splosh" of the friendly blue sea as she kissed the hulls of this sleepy armada.

My friend saw none of this. Like so many others today, who seek the "good life" with all of their energies while it slips "unnoticed" through their fingertips. He had lost himself in the "mechanics" of building his business. The tranquil beauty that was his for the taking no longer held any interest for him. How easily we "trap" ourselves into pursuing that which is already ours. Our attitudes become "fixed" over a period of time; and, by degrees of change which are "ever so small", we awaken one day to find that the elaborate machinery that we have constructed to help us achieve our dreams — now holds us prisoner.

The larger attitude signs are not always as readily discernable as the more obvious "character traits" but the damage that occurs as a result of these unfortunate flaws can be seen in many places.

The child of the "successful" businessman who hardly knows his Father.

The long-suffering wife who has played second fiddle to a "profession" for many years.

The mother or father who has "lost" their son or daughter to ambition, and would settle "in a minute" for a personal visit by that loved one, as opposed to another newspaper article telling about "how well they are doing."

Our priorities, like our attitudes, oftentimes become confused as we run the race of life; and it is sadly true, that we seldom appreciate the really "great" things in life — until they are gone from us forever.

Following closely upon the heels of such a loss, there comes a severe attack of "self-punishing guilt." This can be, and often is, one of the deadliest kinds of suffering that a human being will ever have to endure. The effect upon the long-term attitude can be ruinous. The soul is racked by feelings of guilt because of thoughtlessness, inconsideration, and the ommision of simple little kindnesses that should have been shown, but unfortunately — were not. The bearer of this burden often loses confidence in his or her own self-worth. It is difficult to believe in yourself if you feel that you have somehow betrayed those whom you love the most.

A strange, insatiable desire to "punish" oneself, will often manifest itself in the attitude of persons thus afflicted. It is clear that a life spent in the pursuit of "self-sabotage" is one that is doomed to unproductive unhappiness. There is one cure . . . and **only** one.

The answer lies in the total, and complete, forgiveness of oneself. A realistic and totally honest appraisal of the shortcomings and shortsightedness of the human animal, will inevitably reveal us to be creatures far less perfect than the angels.

There is a gap, like the Grand Canyon, between our intentions and our actions. Therefore, we must forgive ourselves, learn from our mistakes, and move on. A good friend of mine, and sometimes poet, has said it best. With his permission, I will share with you his philosophy — and his poem.

LOOK AHEAD

Think about the future,
Keeping current matters first.
Looking back may cause you grief
And remind you of the worst.
Don't wallow in past events
That are beyond your reach,
Instead, remember past mistakes,
And the lessons that they teach.
Don't dwell upon endearments gone,
Those thoughts just make you sad,
Look upon the brighter side,
Priceless things can still be had.
Everyone has made mistakes,
You're not the only one.
Forgive yourself — and others too,
The future's just begun.

Mack Finseth
Santa Barbara

CHAPTER FOUR

THE DREAM CRUSHER

It's always a chore for me to write about negative, depressing subjects. I have learned over the years not to allow myself to think in negative terms because *thoughts are things*. I believe that the person who dwells upon the possible misfortunes that *might* occur in their life is, in fact, inviting the manifestation of those fears by granting them *the right to life*. To put it another way, the only control you have over an otherwise uncontrollable situation, in my opinion, is the strength of your faith, hope, and unshakable belief that *everything will turn out all right*. Scientifically, arguments could be made to the effect that there is no positive way to prove that the strength of one's belief has any effect whatsoever on the outcome of the affairs of men. I must, however, strenuously support the concept—and my own conviction—that they do.

When science has taken its best shot and failed, when learned men of medicine have struggled valiantly and lost, when the collective efforts of knowledge have been applied without success, the day is often won by some lone, courageous figure who has wielded as their only weapon **the strength of their faith**. The *attitude* which has formed itself without the benefit of this miraculous ingredient is incomplete. We have been told numerous times that it will "be unto us according to our *faith*." How then can we hope to achieve the dreams of our individual lives if we cannot **believe** in those things which we cannot see? — Far more dreams have been crushed by lack of *faith*, than by lack of money.

Who was it who said, "be careful what you set your heart

upon—for you shall surely have it"? I believe that those wise words carry with them a warning. If your attitude is influenced by the negative belief that "the worst that can happen probably will"—correct it at once. You are *inviting* the worst by giving it power—*your belief* that it can happen.

I marvel at the extent to which persons of uncommon charm, ability, and natural good looks will sometimes go to *offset* those advantages by conducting themselves in a manner which *turns away* the success that could easily be theirs. Having been told repeatedly throughout their lives that they "had it made," they seem to be determined to prove that "everything is against them." The fear of not living up to expectations sends them scurrying through life seeking legitimate reasons for failure.

When we speak of *bad attitudes* and the reasons for them, we are covering a lot of territory indeed. In no way can we hope to cover the subject in any depth in the extent of these few pages. We can, however, recognize the fact that "bad attitude" is a **dream crusher** and an enemy. Perhaps through this realization we can learn to search out the causes of our own shortcomings and, hopefully, to be on the alert for "chinks in our own armour" with an eye towards correcting them before they do us harm.

I think it's important at this point that we draw a few distinctions concerning our attitudes. Let's define some of the "gray areas" so we will know what we are observing in the future.

To Learn a Man's True Nature Study His Attitudes.

From what has gone before in this book, we know that there are attitude signs to be read, that our attitudes have been formed from many sources, and that the results of our attitudes can and will affect the remainder of our lives in a most prolific way. What we must guard against, at this point, is the possibility of *misreading* the attitudes of some, thereby becoming guilty of judging our fellow man *wrongly*. With that thought in mind, let's investigate a few different forms of attitude.

The Dream Crusher

Attitude Clash

Supposing you get up one morning and the sun is shining beautifully, the birds have begun their morning serenade, and you can taste the goodness of life all about you. The morning coffee is excellent, the mailman whistling cheerfully brings you a refund check from your income taxes, and the world outside your home on the way to work, seems packed with people wearing friendly, handsome faces.

You stride purposefully into work, determined to "get a real handle on it today." Your fellow employees are helpful and pleasant, and you begin to feel as though "life isn't half so bad after all." — Then the boss arrives. He slams into his office with a chip on his shoulder and immediately makes a phone call in a loud angry voice that can be heard audibly through his closed office door. A few minutes later he throws open the door and, in a strong roar akin to that of a wounded polar bear, summons you to his lair. If you're part of the human race, your first reaction will be—Oh, Oh!

The short walk to his office reminds you a lot of your first trip to the dentist. Once inside, you suddenly realize how David must have felt when he was introduced to Goliath. The boss launches into a full scale attack on civilization, his ex-wife, the government, and finally his employees. Throughout the duration of this tense outburst, you find your own anger growing inside your chest like a miniature hot air balloon.

A few moments ago you were at peace with the world, now your peaceful attitude has been gobbled up by the infectious nature of an *angry* attitude. The course of events that will follow is almost predictable. You will probably bark back at the boss; he will in turn snap at his other employees. **YOU** will start speaking sharply to those with whom you come into contact, and before the day is over, you will just want to get the hell out of there.

What has taken place here is **attitude clash**. The important thing to remember when you're involved in one of these confrontations is the fact that you are dealing with *reactionary* attitude and **not** normal attitude. It's no secret that many people who are normally "nice guys" can turn into something completely different when reacting to pressures, anger, bad news, or other unpleasant experiences. Just for the sake of exploration, let's assume that the boss is really a "super nice guy." His concern for the welfare of his employees has been outstanding; he always has something a little "extra" for you at Christmas time; more than once he has jumped in to rescue one of your fellow workers from a financial calamity; and, under normal circumstances, he's just a "sweetheart" of a guy to work for—what happened??

Well—while you were drinking that great cup of coffee this morning—he got a phone call—from the Internal Revenue Service. They want to see his records for the last four years. Then his ex-wife's lawyer called to inform him that she was going to drag him back into court to get her alimony payments raised. On top of that, the mailman showed up with an outrageous bill from the dentist for his daughter's braces.

He jumped into his car, determined to escape from this madhouse with his sanity intact, and promptly backed over the mailbox. The drive to work was to him an exercise in "nut dodging." Every ding-dong in the world seemed to be on the road and "out to get him." By the time he arrived at the office, he was just about ready for a trip to "Happy Valley" himself. This then— is the pathetically "set upon" individual who arrives at work.

It might have worked out all right in spite of this tragicomic beginning, if you had not had the misfortune of finding the parking lot full upon your entering this morning—except for *his* space. You may remember thinking, "he won't mind" and "there will be a space by the time he gets here." Unfortunately—he did, and there wasn't.

As unpalatable as *attitude clash* can be, we are guilty of a serious error in judgment when we allow ourselves to get caught up in the passion of the moment, and to form harsh opinions concerning the *"true"* attitude of those persons who demonstrate by their "out of character" actions that "something is not quite right here."

Rightfully, we should learn to recognize the *reactionary attitude*, and then to realize that words spoken in anger, or under the strain of pressures unknown to us, are not to be taken seriously—not to be remembered. The mature approach to this problem is a mixture of compassion and control, somewhat like the following:

ONE: Remember what the person is **really** like.

TWO: Realize that they are **hurting** in some way.

THREE: Try to calm them in a pleasant, understanding way.

FOUR: Refuse to allow yourself to become *infected* with their anger, despondency, fear, or whatever.

FIVE: Do not accept anything said to you or about others as indications of their true feelings; these are the words of **passion**—not truth.

SIX: Let the whole affair end with you—do not allow it to grow.

Attitude clash is a common occurrence, not confined to any particular set of circumstances. It happens between mother and daughter, father and son, husband and wife, friend and friend. In any situation where two or more people are gathered, the possibility of attitude clash exists. It is as broad in scope as is the human experience. Diversity of background, religion, politics, mood, health, or even the weather can be fertile ground for attitude clash. The solution to the wearisome distress that it generates lies somewhere in the realization that a *healthy attitude* must contain, as one of its prime ingredients a strong, almost reverent, respect for *the other person's point of view*. If we can learn to value flexibility over stubborn pride—human concern over concrete dogma—an ear that listens over a mouth that asserts, then perhaps at last we shall have abandoned the caves of despair in favor of a land of plenty where the *need to be right*, is replaced by an effort to be tolerant.

Fluctuations in attitude are, of course, bound to occur in all of our lives. The hi's and low's of mood, mental strength, physical well-being, and countless other factors combine in an incongruous hodgepodge of emotional influence to direct our actions and reactions on any given day — or hour. There is little we can do, in most cases, for someone who is beset by an unfavorable combination of these elements other than to "mend our own fences" by practicing a little old fashioned empathy.

The *problem*, which comes neatly packaged along with our deep set convictions, is a kind of *mental blindness*. We permit the ideas, opinions, and points of view of other persons to penetrate our own thoughts only insofar as they do not disturb in any way those things which we have at some point in our lives accepted as being true. We rarely pause to *question* our own beliefs. The greatest good we can do another in the exchange of ideas is to present to them the gift of *recognition*. Let it be known to them, that you value their thoughts, if only because "they thought of them."

The Merry-Go-Round

The *dream crusher* (bad attitude) is insidious in nature and like most evils it comes subtly clothed in a wide assortment of disguises. It can pass undetected as "wry humor," a "what the hell" attitude, lighthearted-irreverence, or resentment of authority. It shuns responsibility and jibes pitilessly at sacred institution and personal misfortune alike. We are speaking, of course, of the more *advanced* cases of bad attitude. The bearers of these traits are those about whom it is often said — "They're their own worst enemy." The truth of that statement can easily be seen in the *quality* of their lives. They climb aboard a *merry-go-round* of cause and effect that spins them irrevocably in a pointless whirl of frustration and wasted dreams. The relationship between *bad attitude* and *bad habits* and *bad lives* can be seen everywhere if we but look and reflect. It is ironic in the extreme, that the badly warped attitude which has conditioned itself to "set snares" for, or ridicule the efforts of, other human beings will, in the end, inevitably suffer at the hands of its own construction. The very same attitude that directs our actions toward others, controls — I said *controls* — our actions concerning ourselves. No wonder, then, that we "reap what we sow" in spite of our efforts to the contrary.

Once a bad attitude has entrenched itself in the makeup of a man or a woman, there is a peculiar *spontaneity* that sets in, driving them relentlessly down the path of self-destruction. It is as though forces of great power had gathered at the point of weakness, in order to exploit and enlarge upon the evils spawned by this devious demon. — And I suspect that this is not too distant from the truth.

A *bad attitude* is an open door to bad habits. — John drinks because he is unhappy with his job. This in turn causes him to perform badly at work, which in turn causes the boss to dislike him, which rattles his confidence and makes him fearful of losing his job, which causes him to anesthetize his fears at the nearest bar. Thusly he finds himself aboard — *the merry-go-round.*

Peggy has never been very popular. She has compensated for all of the missed dates and parties that her friends attend by *rewarding herself* with food. As a result, she has become extremely overweight, and now finds it harder than ever to get a date. Her appetite for all manner of pastries and sweets has almost become an obsession. The source of her problem in the beginning was her lack of popularity. But now her *alternate compensation* has in itself become a problem — which drives her farther and farther from the popularity that she so desperately craves. She is also aboard — *the merry-go-round.*

The *attitude flaw* which originally precipitated the conduct of both John and Peggy was an inability to "face up" to their respective problems in a mature, confident manner. Had John taken the bull by the horns at the outset, he probably could have resolved his difficulties at work, or at least made preparations for a career change in a thoughtful, organized fashion — maybe even improving his position in the process. Peggy, on the other hand, had a weight problem complicated by a loss of self-esteem. If she had chosen to *do something* about it, like mapping out a campaign to overcome both her obesity and her lack of social grace, the end results may have been surprising indeed.

Unhappily, both John and Peggy chose to *withdraw* from the realities of their problems and opted instead to *escape* by means of temporary pleasures, rather than seeking bonafide solutions. The journey upon which they have now embarked is fraught with danger. John may find that his *escape* one day becomes his captor. Peggy will face serious health problems, along with her growing resentment against her own person, unless she can find the strength to alter the course of her life by discarding all forms of *self deception*, pinpointing the real reasons for her unhappiness, and then "attacking" them with unbridled *faith* in the outcome.

We are all creatures of our own belief. Let us take great care, then, to believe in ourselves and in the things that we would aspire to, without reservation. Permit no man, regardless of his station in life, to steal away from you the spark of achievement. You were created, whomever you are, with a little touch of God inside of you. You will rise to the heights of your possibilities in one way only — by *reaching* — and *reaching* — and *reaching*.

The *degrees* of bad attitude are as numerous as are the peoples of the earth. In addition to the "serious" attitude problems possessed by many, lesser afflictions are all too commonplace. The bad attitude will feed upon its own folly and render as "useless" otherwise helpful information that could contribute to the betterment of the person involved. We learn to spot the more significant *icebergs* of a poor attitude and to hang labels on people as a result of our observations. Unseen, however, is the great mass of conflict hovering silently beneath the surface. We give names to the "tips" of the icebergs — know-it-all attitude — stubborn attitude — persecution attitude — one-upmanship attitude — holier-than-thou attitude. — The list goes on and on.

What we have no way of knowing is the extent to which these — —"minor" attitude problems have affected the lives of those who are thus afflicted. How many friends have they lost? How many opportunities have slipped through their fingers because somebody didn't like them? How many times have they turned away a helping hand because of the bruskness of their demeanor? One thing is clear. The *self* that you project to others will without fail prompt the reaction you will receive. If you occasionally have those days when everybody that you come in contact with seems to be mad at the world, look to your own projections. The chances are better than fair, that you're wearing your "grouch face." If, on the other hand, everyone has a friendly smile and a pleasant greeting — You're doing just fine — don't change a thing.

Evolving Gracefully

There are monumental changes in the cycle of life that, oftentimes, catch us unawares. The impact of these changes affect some people to a much greater degree than others. Age changes, for example, are slid into and out of very comfortably by some persons, while others go through genuine discomfort and, in some cases — serious trauma.

If a person is afraid of dying, as many people are, or for some reason has acquired a fear of growing old, the changes at 30— 40—or—50 can be fearful experiences for them. Their *attitude* concerning the aging process will "set the tone" for their reactions.

One young woman may arise on the morning of her thirtieth birthday amid loud proclamations about how "old" she is getting. **"My God, do you realize that I'm thirty years old today??** The twenty's are **gone**, the teenage years are **gone**, it's all passing by so quickly — Oh God — **Thirty!!** " Of course, it escapes her entirely that "God willing" she still has her thirty's, forty's, fifty's, sixty's, seventy's, and quite possibly, her eighty's to look forward to. The emphasis is on *what she has lost*, not what she still has to enjoy. Another lady may arise on the morning of her *eightieth* birthday and cheerfully remind everyone that she is only "one day older" than she was yesterday. Put in this fashion, it really doesn't seem like such a big deal. The difference, of course, is that some persons view the anniversary of their birth as a *signal* that life is swiftly passing them by, and that they had better get out and **do** something before it's too late. This type of unreasonable panic is unfortunately the cause of an alarming amount of stress to both the "fearful person" and to other close family members as well. It is sadly true that these *significant* anniversaries are often followed closely by "family troubles" and an unusually high incidence of divorce.

We fail to grasp the enormity of the ambivalent waves of confusion suffered by some of our fellow human beings unless or until we experience a similar situation. Other high points or, depending upon the point of view, low points in the cycle of life can cause a like amount of distress for some people. The last child leaves home — Mother now feels as though her life has no purpose, (empty nest syndrome). Dad closes the doors for the last time on the business he built from scratch — he now feels useless. Young Bill Jones is released from the service after four years — he finds it extremely difficult to adjust to civilian life. Jenny Smith is told by her boss and lover that "it's all over" — she is now thirty-eight and unmarried. Tom Benson (age 55) is fired by the new boss (age 26) after 25 years with the company.

As cataclysmic as these happenings may appear to be on the surface, I do **not** believe that they should be permitted to wreck lives. The point of view is all important here. Allow yourself a few days of anger, remorse, guilt, pity, or whatever, but then *get on with your life*. It isn't over — not by a damn site. It is merely time to reconstruct — that's all.

The key to *evolving gracefully* when undergoing major transitions in your life is simply this — focus in on the **positive** aspects of the situation and look with cheerful anticipation towards the **future**. It is not the enormous **size** of these problems (real or imagined) that is so frightening. It is the **fear of the unknown**, coupled with a tendency to focus on the *negative* side of the occurrence that really causes the panic. We punish ourselves by dwelling upon whatever it was that we lost. Our thoughts concerning the future are too often limited to a plaintive cry of "where do I go from here??"

Yes, I know that some of you may be thinking — Oh sure, Rog., "Look for the silver lining." Right? Wrong! I am not overlooking for a moment the serious concern that any normal person would be bound to feel when faced with a sizeable lifestyle change. I know you won't be dancing in the streets or whistling "Happy days are here again" as you try to put the pieces back together again. I **do** know, however, that you should be looking for the benefits which are now in your **favor** as the result of that lifestyle change.

Every major alteration in the status quo of your own particular lifestyle situation carries with it, the seeds of a new and exciting experience, as yet unexplored. Just over the horizon from "that which is ended" lies the beautiful *garden of new beginnings*, where all things are fresh and green. There are new friendships waiting to grow—new challenges waiting for your own special touch—new and interesting people unlike any you have met in the past. A whole new world awaits *your presence* in order to be complete. We tend to behold the closing of chapters in our lives as endings—they are not. They are merely "rest stops." We have but to turn the pages in order to get on with our own individual stories.

The mother who sadly watches her last child leave home should *rejoice* in a job well done and then search her mind for those long suppressed desires that were denied her during the child rearing years. Perhaps she always wanted to paint, sculpt, or travel—what a wonderful time in her life to do those things.

And father, who closed the doors on his business feeling like an old horse put to pasture—how priceless his knowledge could be to those younger persons struggling fearfully up the ladder of accomplishment. And now at last he can devote time to polishing his golf game, refining his fishing skills, or other enjoyable pastimes that he never had the time for—until now.

In cases of extreme personal loss, such as that which was suffered by Jenny Smith, or Tom Benson, the cure remains the same except for one important difference. *Grievous loss*, if left to fester, can easily become the source of physical, and in some cases mental, deterioration. For that reason an effort must be made to *get moving in a new direction* as hastily as possible. As cold as it may sound, the greatest remedy for an unhappy ending to a love affair, is the active pursuit of a new love. The surest cure for a boss who doesn't appreciate you—is one who does.

It has to do with *replacing* that which is lost with something of *greater* value. Hindsight is truly a great teacher. Rarely in the course of human events do we look back over our shoulders after a reasonable period of time has passed and bemoan our losses. We are by nature *goal striving creatures*, and the resiliency that has enabled mankind to rise above the "onslaughts of the ages", is as much a part of our makeup as is our ability to think. As Winston Churchill once said, "Do you think we've come all this way because we are made of sugar candy?"

The implacable mountains of difficulty, the unfordable streams of despair, the great chasms of personal loss, and the endless ocean of human affliction, all—yes, all—melt away like insignificant pussycats before the boundless, magnificent courage of the human spirit. This then is the great *superweapon* which was gifted to you by the Almighty, that you might withstand, contend with, and ultimately subdue, the forces of evil that are arrayed against you. It would be nice if all forms of evil showed up dressed in a devil's uniform with horns, a tail, and the slight smell of something burning. Unfortunately, we usually spend large chunks of our lives dealing with the "devious disguises" of evil before we finally learn to recognize it for what it is.

Magnetic Conditioning

It has been said that "we wear on our faces what we are."

Although there is some truth to the statement, it is in reality a blatant over-generalization. It is fact, however, that our personal appearances will in many instances *draw unto us*, like an invisible magnet, a strong reflection of the attitude we project. Let me see if I can't clarify that statement somewhat. Let's imagine for the moment that you have a friend who is inclined towards frowning a great deal. In addition to that, he is by nature a bit on the shy side and not given to lengthy dialogue. The image that he would probably project is that of a sour faced grouch who isn't very friendly. Although that may not really be the case at all, the prolonged *reflective-reactions* he receives will, over a period of time, cause him to view others as grouchy, unfriendly, and even untrustworthy. This will in turn cause **him** to become grouchy, unfriendly, and suspicious of others. When the day finally arrives that he *sees* himself as he thinks others see him, the man will at that point *match the face*. This then is *magnetic conditioning*— the act of drawing to oneself the reflection of what is projected until, in the end, you **become** what you have projected.

Let's view the other side of the spectrum. Pretend that you have another friend who is totally opposite from the first fellow. This guy is Mr. All American. He has a million dollar smile, everybody loves him, and he projects the image of an intelligent, friendly, young man who is really going places. The *feedback* he receives from his teachers at school, his friends, his summertime employers, in fact everybody he comes in contact with, serves to *reinforce* what he has projected. With this kind of positive verification, it's a pretty safe bet that he will *believe* what he has projected, and in the end he will *become* the man who fits the face. From this perspective, we can easily see the wisdom in the ancient golden rule, "Do unto others as you would have them do unto you."

The person I **really** want to talk about is Mr. Average. This could be you, me, or most of our respective friends. This is the person who has neither great natural good looks, nor a face that would stop a clock; he is *Everybody* U.S.A. His features are ordinary; therefore, he must rely solely upon his *attitude* if he is to present a favorable projection, and in turn receive the benefits of its reflection.

The two individuals we have just discussed are at opposite ends of the scale, but the really interesting people fall somewhere in between the two. For example, there's a person who is "slightly on the unattractive side", but through the sheer force of his *personality* and *sense of humor* (both are ingredients of a healthy attitude) he projects an image of friendliness and trustworthiness which causes you to ignore completely his physical appearance. There are also those persons who have suffered some physical impairment which, in the visual sense, causes them to be **very** unattractive. Still, a small amount of exposure to their charm, consideration for others, and (for want of a better word) *class*, leads you to view them as persons concealing some hidden source of greatness beneath the surface appearance.

What we are actually seeing here is *attitude* at its best. The significant lesson to be learned is the inescapable certainty that it is the **attitude** that makes the person, and **not** the physical appearance. I want to enlarge upon that statement to this extent. It is true that some people become whatever it is that they become through *magnetic conditioning*, as illustrated in the two earlier cases we have discussed. But the point I wish to make crystal clear is this—had they possessed the strength and hardiness of a healthy attitude, their physical appearance, whether good or bad, would have been **secondary** to their attitude, and in that capacity could **not** have substantially contributed to the end result. The bottom line lies in the realization that "beauty is only skin deep."

The true measure of a man or a woman is found in the strength of their character, as witnessed to by their *attitudes*, and not in the package it all comes in. Now, for the sake of easing the journey through life, common sense will dictate that you "make the most of what you've got." It is certainly not in your best interest to dress in a slovenly fashion, ignore the rules of personal hygiene, or otherwise disregard a manner which states, "I care what you think of me." The absence of this consideration will leave you *open* to the negative possibilities of *magnetic conditioning*. In short—if **you** don't care what you are, other people will soon be treating you in a way that expresses the same lack of concern for you, that you have shown for yourself. A healthy attitude is accompanied by a genuine concern for "what others think of you." The opposite posture is an "advertisement" that you have no particular pride in yourself, nor do you value their opinions **of** you. This sort of projection cannot be expected to rally them to your cause. A distinction should be made between *physical appearance* and *personal appearance* at this point. Your physical appearance is that over which you have little, or no control. Your "personal" appearance has to do with all of those things, that it is within your power to alter, improve, embelish upon, or control.

Ellen Powell

Since we obviously would not consciously choose to become victims of adverse *magnetic conditioning*, let's probe a little deeper into the workings of this strange phenomenon and see if we can discover how to avoid it. Think with me now. Envision, if you will, a middle-aged woman walking into a doctor's office. She is wearing ordinary, but nice appearing clothes. Her expression is passive, and offers no clue as to what her attitude is like. You are merely an observer, so you have no particular reason to either like or dislike this person. She steps up to the reception desk, and in a clear but passionless voice, asks to see Dr. Jones.

Duty Nurse: Do you have an appointment Madam?

Lady: No, but he'll want to see me.

Duty Nurse: Well, the doctor is really busy today. May I have your name, please?

Lady: Tell him Mrs. Powell is here, and please tell him that I don't have much time.

Duty Nurse: He's with a patient right now. Would you like to have a seat?

Lady: Well, just tell him I'm here will you?

Duty Nurse: Yes Ma'am, I'll tell him.

Up to this point, you have been quietly reading a magazine while awaiting your own turn to see the Doctor. Without looking up you subconsciously decide that there is something about this person that you don't like. Now you casually raise your eyes to give her the once over. What you see is a fairly attractive woman who smiles briefly as your eyes meet hers. She is wearing a substantial amount of jewelry, and for some reason that you don't really think about, this also annoys you.

She finally takes a seat and searches quickly through the pile of magazines on the stand next to her end of the couch; she selects a copy of *Fashion Beautiful* to thumb through. This also bothers you, somehow. A few minutes later the good doctor appears and smiles in her direction, "Would you step this way, Mrs. Powell," he says. She stands abruptly and swishes off into one of the patient rooms, the good doctor trailing behind her like an obedient puppy. Now you're **SURE** you don't like her. As you sit awaiting the reappearance of this abrasive person, your subconscious mind is prodding you gently about the *unfair* manner in which she gained entrance to the doctor, ahead of you.

When at last she re-emerges on her way to the street exit, you do **not** return her quick smile . . . you don't like her. Why?

Let's pause right there for a moment. At the beginning of this chapter we mentioned the possibilities that abound for *wrongly* judging our fellow man (or woman). We easily jump to conclusions concerning other persons about whom we know very little or nothing. It is **we** who are in the wrong when we allow preprogrammed impressions, prejudices, and tastes to color our discernment as we attempt to apply the art of *instant attitude readings*. We must remember that this practice is primarily for our benefit and protection, and is **not** meant to be a system by which we can make judgments or condemnations based upon the flimsy evaluations that can be constructed from the limited amount of material available to us in such instances.

In the interests of fair play, I would like to return to the scene just described, only this time we will try to "clearly understand" what it is we are seeing.

Forgive me as I again use *you* as the observer. Obviously, my purpose for that is to permit you to *feel* the scenario as much as is possible under these conditions.

As the lady in our story steps up to the reception desk, you find yourself slightly offended because she does not cheerfully engage the receptionist in a lighthearted inquiry as to when the doctor will be free—as you would have done. The exchange which takes place between the duty nurse and our lady, comes across to you as though she were endowed with an uncommon amount of "self-importance." This offends you, also.

As your eyes meet hers, the smile she gives you seems lifeless and insincere. You feel almost as if she were patronizing you. The clothing she is wearing does not impress you as being that of an "important" person. This contradiction strikes you as being somehow deceitful. Although you don't *consciously* think about it, you have appraised her ample amount of jewelry and found it to be inexpensive and not at all in keeping with that which should be worn by someone who can waltz in and see the doctor—without an appointment. Your dislike of this person is compounded by the fact that she then chooses a magazine to read which you know to be filled with "costly" fashion model clothing—beyond your means, and as your computers have now told you—beyond hers. Again, the impression you have formed of her, is one of someone who is putting on a false front, and who has little consideration for the rights of others. The "last straw" is when the doctor invites her in ahead of you, without any kind of explanation. Being a person of reasonable social grace, you accept all of this without complaint. But you withhold your smile from her as she leaves. Too bad—she could have used that smile.

Through the wonders that writers are permitted, I'm going to introduce you to this strangely abrasive lady. Her name is **Ellen Powell**. Three years ago she had undergone an operation for cancer of the female organs. It was a frightening period in her life during which time, she had fought the spread of the dread disease most valiantly. The surgery was followed by a long period of chemotherapy, radiation treatments and assorted experimental procedures which finally culminated in the "checking" of the disease, at least temporarily—until now. She had lost all of her hair during the procedure, her husband of eighteen years had deserted her for a younger woman, unable to cope with the terrible strain placed upon the family throughout the lengthy ordeal. The long and hard battle had been punctuated by episodes of "near death" and "ominous predictions." Uncommon courage had been the deciding factor which had pulled Ellen through those horrible days. She had reached deep within herself to call upon the strength that is born of despair—for the sake of her children, and for the sake of numerous other people whom she had met in the hospital, who had drawn upon her fortitude to sustain them throughout their own frightful days.

Last Thursday, Ellen had come in for her semi-annual checkup. The doctor discovered a large lump in her breast. Tests were made, and it was decided than an immediate biopsy should be performed, in an effort to determine if they were again dealing with a malignant growth. The doctor had spoken to her in his most serious, dictatorial tone. "Now, Ellen, I want you to be in here on Wednesday without fail. The results will be back from the lab by then and we will have to decide on a course of action." She had responded with a protest, and a frightened look on her face. "But Doctor, I feel fine. This thing hasn't bothered me, and besides that, Wednesday is my day in the children's nursery at pre-school." "Ellen," he had replied, "you of all people should know that this is nothing to fool around with. Now I want you in here Wednesday, and no excuses." "But I absolutely have to be at the nursery; there's no one to take my place," she implored. The doctor's face was grim. "Stop by on your way to the nursery. Just go to the desk and tell the duty nurse that you're here. I'll come right out, and we'll talk about it. You can be on your way in five minutes." Reluctantly—she had agreed.

The following few days were a nightmare. Ellen wasn't at all sure that she could survive another hospital stay, and the spector of losing one of her breasts, or worse, had opened up a whole new chamber of horrors for her, which caused her to break down and cry at the most inopportune times. She had met one of her oldest friends for lunch and a bit of shopping on the day following her visit to the doctor. While they were awaiting their order at a small restaurant in the shopping mall, she had begun sobbing uncontrollably. It just hit her all at once, without any warning. Her friend was dismayed and confused; Ellen hadn't mentioned her fears to anyone. Together, they left the restaurant without awaiting the lunch they had ordered. There were several episodes like that in the few days following.

When the day arrived for her appointment with the doctor, she had risen early, and taken extra pains with her personal appearance. As she dressed that morning, she tried bravely not to allow herself to stare into the mirror any longer than was necessary. But always there was the great fear that she might never again see herself as the whole person that she was on this day. Perhaps out of indulgence for herself, she carefully placed her favorite pieces of jewelry on her person; she didn't seem to notice that she had assembled a goodly amount.

She prayed silent prayers as she drove to the doctor's office. When she found it necessary to use the brake, she noticed consciously that her legs were shaking. After cautiously parking the car, she walked into the doctor's office on rubbery legs, wishing to herself that she had not worn her high heels. Her eyes were misty, and for a moment she found it necessary to pause and blink away the intruding tears. At the reception desk she struggled to keep her voice steady, as she asked to see the doctor. "Is Doctor Jones in?"

Duty Nurse: "Do you have an appointment, Madam?"

Ellen Powell: "No, but he'll want to see me."

Duty Nurse: "Well, the doctor is really busy today, may I have your name, please?"

Ellen Powell:	"Tell him Mrs. Powell is here, and please tell him that I don't have much time."
Duty Nurse:	"He's with a patient right now, would you like to have a seat?"
Ellen Powell:	"Well, just tell him I'm here will you?"
Duty Nurse:	"Yes, Ma'am, I'll tell him."

As Ellen turns to find a seat her eyes meet yours. She smiles briefly, and then walks to a place at the end of the couch. After seating herself, she begins to shakily glance through the magazines. In *Fashion Beautiful* she discovers a lovely blue dress that for a brief moment delights her. "I have always looked good in blue—or at least—I used to." Her eyes begin to mist over, and she is on the verge of losing control as the doctor appears. "Would you step this way, Mrs. Powell," he says. Gratefully Ellen leaps to her feet and heads swiftly for one of the patient rooms, brushing past the doctor, barely able to see through her tear washed eyes. The doctor follows her in and closes the door. Once in the seclusion of the small room, Ellen breaks down. "It's bad news isn't it, doctor? I'm going to have to go through the whole mess again aren't I?" Doctor Jones answers softly— compassionately. "Sit down for a moment, Ellen, I want you to understand completely what it is that we're dealing with here." Ellen lowered herself into one of the two small wicker chairs and confronted the doctor with her gaze. Doctor Jones took a position, half sitting, half leaning against the lone gurney in the center of the room. He removed his glasses slowly— purposefully—and crossed his arms loosely across his chest. "Ellen," he said, "I don't want to give you the impression that what we've found is not serious — on the other hand, there is genuine cause for optimism." He hesitated, as if to choose his words very carefully. "The lab report shows that there is a small concentration of malignant cells. It also shows that they don't seem to be spreading, and that they're apparently confined to an isolated area of the breast." He waited patiently for the question that he knew would come. "Does this mean I'll have to lose my breast?" she said. "It means that we will have to operate immediately, and Ellen, I **mean** immediately," he said insistantly. "There is no way of knowing what we will find once inside the breast, but if all goes well, thanks to new techniques that weren't available even two years ago, we may—I said **may**— be able to save the breast. But understand me clearly, Ellen; every day that you delay, reduces that likelihood substantially." He paused briefly to allow his words to sink in. "I want you to give me permission to schedule you for surgery **tomorrow**." Ellen stood slowly; when she answered, her voice was low and shaky. "Sure—why not." She walked towards the door and then turned to face the doctor. "I'm going home now to — try to get my affairs in order. I'll check into the hospital at about 2:00 in the afternoon. I want to spend the morning with my children." She placed her hand on the door knob and turned to speak once more. "Tell me something, doctor — Why me? — What the hell did I ever do to **anybody**?" There was no reply. Ellen walked slowly through the reception room on the way to her car. There was one lone person waiting to see the doctor. She forced a friendly smile. Again there was no reply.

I have told you the story of Ellen Powell for a number of reasons, not the least of which is the clearing of my own conscience. Ellen Powell is a real person, although that is not her name. I know of these events because the doctor is a golfing friend of mine, and our paths were destined to cross many times in the years to come. I learned her true story—and a sobering lesson in humility. You see—**I** was the observer in the reception room—not you. And my preoccupation with *attitude readings* had caused me to misjudge this remarkable lady in a most unfair manner. I shall not soon forget the lessons of that experience. At an earlier point in this book I made reference to the fact that we should use *love* as our guiding light when we practice instant attitude readings. I learned that great truth, from—Ellen Powell.

As I recount these happenings, I find myself strangely fearful of omitting in some way, the full breadth of conclusions that should be drawn from Ellen's story. I see three noteworthy conditions upon which I believe we should spend some time. The first is, of course, the glaringly obvious mistake committed by "yours truly"—that of judging the character of a complete stranger, based solely upon the actions I had observed, with no thought whatsoever for the motivations behind those actions. Lesson Number One, then, should be to "reserve our appraisals of unsavory actions until we have knowledge of the reasons for them." In addition to that, as I have stated a number of times now, we must allow *love* to be our guiding light in any and all attitude readings. How do we do that? I will give you a description of love, and I suspect the answer will become clear to you.

> *Love is patient and kind; love is not jealous or boastful; it is not arrogant or rude. Love does not insist on its own way; it is not irritable or resentful; it does not rejoice at wrong, but rejoices in the right,*
> *Love bears all things, believes all things, hopes all things, endures all things.*
>
> *(1st. Corinthians 13-4 The Holy Bible)*

The second subject that needs further scrutiny is this matter of *magnetic conditioning*. In the case of Ellen Powell, was she in fact drawing unto herself unpleasant reactions from others because of her illness? Even though her "projections" were understandable? The answer is—yes—she was. And perhaps this unhappy fact can serve to illustrate how easily our attitudes can "set the stage" for the *reflective responses* we are apt to receive. No wonder then, that "a day which starts off badly for us has a high 'probability factor' of remaining that way throughout its duration."

My old Dutch grandmother used to absolutely insist that every member of the family began the day with a cheerful "good morning" to everyone present. If we failed in that regard, we could expect a barrage of caustic, nonstop innuendoes designed to assault, in the fullest measure that she could muster, our lack of common courtesy and good manners. We soon learned to start the day with a pleasant "good morning" for everyone within earshot, rather than face the displeasure of this four-foot nine-inch, machette-tongued little Gramma'.

Our choices were simple. Either we started the beginning of

each new day with a bright friendly greeting for our fellow family members — or, Gramma' would screw up the rest of it for us.

In retrospect I can now see the wisdom of launching each day with a happy, cheery greeting. It established the *tone* of our attitudes before we ever left the house, and caused us to *project* the better side of our natures to those with whom we came into contact, thereby *inviting* a like response. Magnetic conditioning has much to do with the *quality* of our days. If our attitude projects hostility, anger, impatience, rudeness or any one of the other hundreds of *negative* frames of mind, the chances of "having a nice day," as the saying goes, are decidedly slim. We will inevitably be the recipients of *reflective reactions* thereby *reinforcing* our foul moods and heaping the hot coals of frustration upon our already fevered dispositions.

On the cheerier side, the opposite is also true. If we sally forth into the midst of each day formidably armed with the "positive" components of a strong, healthy attitude, we most certainly can expect *magnetic conditioning* to function as our friend, solidifying our good thoughts, as we reap the benefits of warm and stimulating reflective reactions.

It is in our own best interest to aid those friends and associates whom we may discern as having slipped into the *negative* patterns of behavior. As we radiate our own "good vibes" to others we are setting up the atmosphere in which **we** will spend the remainder of the day. We ought not try to "talk away" the problems of others. It is tempting to serve up great portions of "philosophical placebos" when one of our friends is distressed, but it is immeasurably more effective to *infect* them with our own great mood. There is nothing as contagious as a *heartfelt laugh*, and the impotence of evil is never laid so bare as when good friends *laugh together* at their own misfortunes.

There is yet another side to the Ellen Powell story, and it would be unforgiveably irresponsible of me to withhold from you, either by oversight, or the fear of appearing "mystic" to some readers, this brightly inspiring aspect of a great lady's character.

It has always seemed to me that we are permitted only brief, tiny glimpses of what heaven must be like while we are here on earth. And yet those minute little insights, in spite of their brevity, can often change forever the nature of our assessments concerning the family of man. The wide, clear eyed innocence of a young child can magically stir within the breast of the most callous examples of mankind, a silent vow to love and protect them no matter what the cost—including life itself.

The sacrifices made by some individuals on behalf of others, for the sheer joy of "giving out of love," often in secret, and without any thought for reward or recognition, can cause us to pause and reflect upon the course of our own ambitions. And the overwhelming courage of certain of our fellow human beings who, for reasons beyond our understanding, are beset with calamity after calamity, and through it all, we find ourselves hard pressed to catch them bemoaning their misfortunes. We find them instead cheerfully encouraging, lifting and strengthening the spirits of others by reason of their unbending faith in the outcome. The "mystery ingredients" that are common to these "uncommon" people can be interpreted to be a "blueprint for success" for the rest of us. A gentle inquisition into the makeup of such persons reveals a simple, yet all encompassing formula which, when fully understood, has the power to arm the possessor against the "furies of Hell" if need be, and to prevail against anything short of that. The formula as I see it is as follows:

FAITH IN GOD
FAITH IN YOURSELF
THE COURAGE TO TRY, AND TRY AGAIN

I was privileged to see this formula in action as the result of knowing Ellen Powell. The following account of those events, it is hoped, will shed further light on the "goodness" that is part of your makeup—and mine, and on the responsibility that we are charged with to "give it away" at every opportunity. Like all truly great possessions, we reap no benefits by owning them — only by sharing them.

Following that dark day at the doctor's office, Ellen checked herself into the hospital in preparation for the surgery that she knew must come.

Through subsequent meetings with Ellen (I was often at the hospital) I began to know her as a "Person". She had come to know me as "Jonesie's Pal" which she later shortened to "J.P." On one occasion I heard that the medication she was taking caused her to be sick to her stomach most of the time, and that she was unable to get a decent night's sleep. I decided to stop by her room to say "Hi." As I poked my head around the corner of the door, I saw her sitting upright in bed, busily knitting some "Little Booties" for her new grandchild. She glanced up over her glasses. "Hi J.P. What's the matter; run out of golf balls?" "No, Ellen, your doctor and mine is off licking his wounds from the sound thrashing I gave him last Thursday. He had some silly excuse about 'performing a triple bypass' today, which probably means he missed the golf ball three times at the practice range and decided not to tangle with me." Ellen smiled lightly, "Oh, I don't know about that J.P. He's pretty devoted to the game. He spends most of his spare time in his office, putting gallstones across the carpet."

At this moment the woman in the bed next to Ellen's began moaning lowly. In one smooth motion Ellen removed her glasses and placed them on the nightstand along with her knitting. With the other hand she threw back the covers of her bed and rolled out to cradle the woman's head in her arms.

Woman:　Oh, Ellen, it hurts so bad.

Ellen:　I know honey, but it'll get better; the worst is over now.

Woman:　What if it doesn't? What if I die; who will take care of my children?

Ellen:　(Her voice was firm) Now you're not going to die, just stop talking like that. You're going to get well soon and go home to your family.

The woman was silent for a moment, and then she spoke softly. "Thanks, Ellen, it's O.K. now—it doesn't hurt so bad."

Ellen: You're sure you're alright?

Woman: Yes.

Ellen: Good—Now try to get some sleep honey—I'll be right here.

Woman: O.K. Ellen—I'll try.

Ellen placed the covers softly over her shoulders as you would a small child, and caressed her hair in gentle, affectionate strokes. Soon the woman was breathing deeply—fast asleep. I watched the concern in her manner and sensed the great trust the woman had placed in Ellen.

After a few minutes Ellen removed herself from the woman's bed and glanced at me. "Sorry J.P., I didn't mean to ignore you," she said. Her face looked a little white. She excused herself momentarily and went into the restroom. I could hear her wretching uncontrollably. When she returned, she slid back into bed and smiled at me through watery eyes. I spoke to her quietly—"Later, Ellen." She winked reassuringly, "Later, J.P."

It was astonishing how Ellen had bounced back from her "bad news" and the surgery that followed, to once again, assume the role of the strong, dependable, unconquerable friend. Others seemed to gravitate to her side automatically when they found that their own strength was ebbing.

The countless kindnesses shown by Ellen during her hospital stay are too numerous to mention, although a few of them stand out in my memory—like the time she hired a Hawaiian group to play music for one of her little friends who was dying. The young man had come from Hawaii originally and had spoken to Ellen often about his boyhood in the Islands. On that last day, when he lay dying, the music had brought a peaceful smile to his face as he slowly slipped away amid pleasant memories of his beloved homeland. Then there was the old lady who boasted constantly about her handsome, successful son who had become a "big shot" with some corporation. Her tales were always laced with excuses about why "he can't come to see me right now because he's so busy." I had the soul stirring privilege of overhearing Ellen's long distance phone call to Mr. "Big Shot." By the time she was through slicing up his pride, the only possible way he could redeem his self-esteem was by grabbing a plane to come see his mother. He did—the next day.

The characteristic that stands out above all the rest in the makeup of Ellen Powell, was her absolutely unshakable belief that everything was going to turn out all right. There were numerous setbacks, frightening medical doubts, professional fears by all concerned—except Ellen. She never doubted—not for a moment—that she would eventually emerge victorious over the fearsome killer that stalked her life. The strength of this conviction carried many others along with her, and made the inevitable easier for those persons whose time had come.

By the way—she did not lose her breast, as she had feared she might, and I believe the tide turned in her favor when she stopped fearing the outcome, and reverted again to her natural state which is, and will always be, that of a fighter who has **Faith In God, Faith In Herself And The Courage To Try, And Try Again.**

One final note: Ellen Powell later remarried—to Doctor Jones. She claims that's the only way she could think of, to get back all that money she had spent on doctor, and hospital bills. . . . What a Gal.

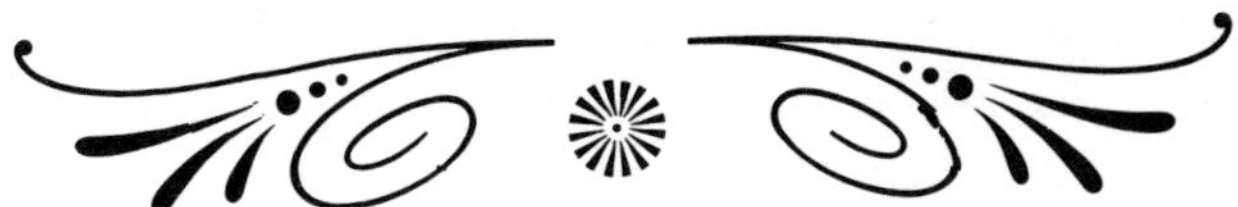

CHAPTER FIVE

ATTITUDE AND YOUR HEALTH

I believe it to be common knowledge that poor physical health will, in the vast majority of instances, affect one's attitude. It's hard to be your "old sweet self" when you are hurting, or suffering the debilitating oppression of fatigue, depression, or any number of other unpleasant physical or mental experiences.

What I would like to examine with you in this chapter, however, is the lesser known fact that "your attitude has an immeasurably important role to play in both the **creation of** your health condition and the **recovery from** destructive physical or mental problems" (as in the case of Ellen Powell).

We have touched upon certain "habit patterns" that lead to unacceptable results in past chapters, so I feel no need to elaborate on those conditions. I do wish to vividly impress upon you though, the extent to which you will determine the status of your own health - by your *attitude*. It is only in recent years that medical science has timidly embraced the concept of "mind over matter" regarding physical condition. Prior to that time, the various forms of "mental conditioning" we could read about were thought largely to be the realm of "self-help advocates", psychics, abstract religious orders, or vaguely understood theories which garnered precious little support from learned men of medicine. I'm happy to say, all of that is changing. As men learn to recognize the validity of the thoughts of others and to cast aside the "blinders" of their own indoctrination, the resultant "sharing of ideas" has produced, and is producing, greatly lengthened strides in man's quest for knowledge.

I read with great interest and satisfaction a recently published article in the Reader's Digest entitled **"Psychosomatic Illness: More than we imagine."** (Reprinted from "Cosmopolitan", October 83). In this article, Dr. William L. Webb, secretary of the Academy of Psychosomatic Medicine, was quoted as saying *"The idea that states of mind, relationships, personalities or lifestyles affect the body is not new, but it has only recently gained the attention of doctors trained in science and technology."* The article then went on to underscore the relationships between heart disease, cancer, stress and other physical problems and the mental conditions thought to be contributory. The author of the article, Catherine Houck, states that *"Evidence is building that suggests emotions play an important part in virtually all illness."*

I couldn't agree more. Perhaps we are on the brink of learning that it is a sickness of the spirit that later manifests itself in physical malfunction that causes our problems, and not the other way 'round.

If this proves to be the case, preventive medicine will undergo a colossal change. The emphasis will then be on the care and training of our *attitudes* rather than the container they come in. If we carry this approach one step farther, we will stumble across the startling discovery that "other persons can effect our health, by affecting our attitudes". The thoughtless son who shouts at his aging mother may be directly contributing to her frailty. The nagging wife who creates an atmosphere of constant spiritual pressure may be in effect shortening the lifespan of her dearest companion - and storing up a life of loneliness for herself. The deeper we look into the implications of this realization, the more we become aware of just how dependent we are, one upon the other. We catch sight of an interdependency far beyond anything we had ever imagined. A balance of nature of the spirit, if you will. Are we our brothers keepers? — Oh, yes!

If we are now ready to admit that our spirits are the "real" part of our makeup, then we must also be willing to seek out and direct our attention towards those things which indicate the "health status" of our individual spirits.

At the beginning of this book, I gave you a description of "attitude". I referred to it as "the window of the soul." Now, I'm well aware that the "eyes" have been called "the windows of the soul," but as many a disappointed lover will tell you, the eyes can tell lies. The attitude, however, when observed over a reasonable period of time, cannot. What better place to focus our inquiry? What characteristic of the family of humans can possibly reflect the condition of the spirit as accurately as can attitude? Learned probing into specific beliefs which make up the attitude, whether they be true or false, whether, real or imagined, fostered by fear or ingrained through education, can only lead to improved spiritual strength, and subsequently to renewed physical health.

We have got to stop lavishing our attention on the condition of the vessel, and start instead to take great care in the making of the wine. Only with this approach shall we begin to produce quality of such excellence that the common "incurables" of our species will no longer have a place in the hearts and minds of men.

Rape, thievery, murder, wanton destruction, and all the rest, begin with the attitude. They are nothing more than the fruits of terribly "warped" attitudes. The culmination of neglected evils allowed to grow without containment until in the end, the spirit is weakened and sickly, and unable to resist. These people then become slaves to their own desires. Captives of their own appetites. Hollow shells of humans devoid of the essence of life. No wonder they return again and again to the plunder of their fellow men, showing no mercy, and displaying no remorse. — They do not possess those things.

The answer will never be found in punishment, incarceration, or the loss of their freedoms. — They have already lost far more than that. The battleground for the spirit of man must be entered into during his early years, before his attitudes become fixed and hard, — before the door to his spiritual strength is slammed shut forever.

It saddens me to say it, but we are all partly to blame — I'm sorry, but it's true. We live in the richest country in the world, but so long as we are willing to tolerate ghetto conditions, or permit the less fortunate to wallow in hopeless situations, we will suffer the results of our own apathy. Those who have been "gutted" of hope repeatedly, will ultimately throw aside restraint and seize whatever they find within their grasp. If you chain up your pet dog for three days and "forget" to feed him, he will probably chase the neighbor's chickens upon his release, with very little thought as to "how *you* will feel about it."

The interdependency which is the proper order of things also extends to our "social" responsibilities. If we continue to turn away from the unpleasant sight of human suffering, we will one day reap the whirlwind of social anarchy. It has begun — it will continue.

There are some who say that you cannot raise these people above their environment. They cite cases where slums have been destroyed and new housing projects erected on the locations. They quickly point out that within the span of a few years, the new buildings begin to look as hideous as did the older homes, with the telltale signs of reckless disregard starkly apparent to all who chance to view them. — That's no surprise. You cannot change the attitudes of these people by the mere act of installing them in surroundings more pleasant to the eye. If you have been raised in an atmosphere where nobody really gives a damn if you spray paint the walls, or break out a window for kicks, or dump your trash wherever you please, you will not automatically alter that behavior just because you have been relocated, or moved into a nicer home. The transfiguration must first take place in the attitude — the spirit if you will, of the inhabitants. The key to the transition lies in the restructuring of the tenants themselves. Education, enlightenment and appreciation for the rights of others as well as a new regard for their own environment.

Some states have found a high success rate in upgrading their slum areas by getting the tenants to participate in the rebuilding process. This approach not only helps to create jobs in the afflicted area, but helps also to create pride in the spirit of all who are involved in the construction of the new neighborhood. It goes against the grain to destroy any part of that which you had a hand in creating. Moreover, man's natural instinct to protect the things he has personally labored for, acts as a safeguard against the irrational behavior of the incorrigible few who would desecrate the handiwork of others with little or no regard for the hours of toil and sweat that went into the project. — A good "right cross" can sometimes do more to change a destructive attitude than many hours of social indoctrination.

The point is: There are ways we can rebuild the lives of our less fortunate citizens, we just have to look a little harder. As George Bernard Shaw once said,

> *Independence? That's middle class*
> *blasphemy. We are all dependent on*
> *one another, every soul of us on earth.*
> *Pygmalion, Act V*

So, the coming together of the haves and have-nots in the common pursuit of social responsibility is best obtained by the participation of all concerned, and not by the patriarchal benevolence of shadowy figures lurking out of sight, and touch behind huge mahogany desks in city councils or banking institutions.

An impossible dream? Perhaps, but I prefer to think that attitudes can be changed if we focus in on the root problems, rather than trying to "spend" our way to a better society. We have led ourselves to believe that we can buy our way out of social problems — we can't. You do not "buy" the hearts and minds of men.

What about the other side of the picture? How do we account for the white collar criminals, the educated con-men, the publicly elected officials who get caught with their hand in the till? We tried so hard to give them all a great start in life, to be sure that they had all of the things that you and I had to do without.

So where did we go wrong? What happened to those wonderful days of yesteryear when nobody bothered to lock their doors?

When friends were our dearest possessions rather than a convenient relationship on our ruthless climb up the ladder of success? Let's roll back the pages of time and review some of the events that have shaped our lives during the past forty-odd years.

Following World War II, a great multitude of our young fighting men returned to this country to find their wives and sweethearts actively engaged in full-time jobs. It had begun as a spirited effort to release the fighting men for duty in the front lines, and to fill those vacancies with a work force of women. Some of you will remember those days, "Rosie the riveter" was one of our idols. The tens of thousands of women who answered the nation's call for help had, and richly deserved, our admiration and gratitude. But a new order of things was in the making. Old traditions had slipped irrevocably beneath the waves of time like an ancient "four master" disappearing from the horizon forever. Many of the returning servicemen found themselves unable to get steady employment. The war effort was winding down and defense plants which had hummed nonstop throughout the brutal conflict, were now beginning to cut back on production, to retool for more peaceful purposes. Many women were laid off, many more sought other employment to keep the home fires burning while their men readjusted to the uncertain economy. As the former warriors found their respective niches, a national trend was taking shape. The two-income family had become a reality for thousands of people, and with it the realization that they could now have many of the things that their forbears had worked a lifetime to possess.

Woman had once again tasted of the forbidden fruit, only this time it was in the form of gainful employment. Whether right or wrong, the growth of the working female population has continued to increase. As of this writing, women comprise 42.6 percent of the work force. The impact that this break from tradition had caused changed the course of our lives for all time. Huge housing developments began to spring up overnight in all sections of the country. The automobile industry suddenly came of age, turning out vast numbers of every conceivable model in its haste to put this new, fast-moving society on wheels. Business was booming everywhere, and the future looked bright and promising. — But we lost something, too.

Mothers, the primary instructors for most of us, were not always around when we needed them. Young people were better fed, better clothed, and better educated than they had ever before been, but they were often left without crucial guidance during the formative years and oftentimes made decisions on their own that affected the remainder of their lives negatively. Yes, I know that this will anger many readers, — but that's the way it was. The guiding hand of reason was not always there to instruct and to enlighten. Mother was often too tired to worry about it when she **was** there. So what did these children see in the attitudes of their parents? They saw them chasing after "things." The emphasis had switched from the strength of one's character to the size of one's bank account. We wound up raising a whole society of professional people whose one and only motivation was **money.** Attorneys would chase down potential clients in an effort to get them to sue somebody. Doctors would perform unnecessary surgery just to receive the fee involved. Politicians and other business people who had once been highly esteemed in our country began to hold hands with men of questionable character.

The great American dream had become the great American grab.

The attitude carried over into the labor unions, management, and every other facet of our economic structure. Soon we were in big trouble. Inflation was eating us alive as we clamored for more of everything. Not a pretty picture. —

Then something happened to jar us back to reality. We suffered through a couple more wars, and a yet newer generation of young people began to make loud noises about our hypocrisy. They were everywhere: demonstrating, singing, pointing a finger at our leaders, accusing us of lies and deceit, and above all, — questioning our *motives* on every front. Where did they come from, this strange generation who had the audacity to confront the old traditional ways in which we did things? Didn't they know this is America, and we always do the right thing here? — They didn't think so. They sprang up before we got fully embroiled in the Vietnam War, and they told us we were wrong. That we had no business over there. — Imagine that.

I've been wanting to say it for a long time, so now I will speak out. These were the children of knowledge. These were the voices of our sleeping heritage. They wore ridiculous clothing, and they let their hair grow far too long to suit us, but they spoke the truth. We later learned just how right they were when we sacrificed thousands of young Americans in an effort to save a corrupt, oppressive regime that had nothing in common with the American way of life at all.

I hope that there will always be a loud chorus of voices in this nation to tell us when we are wrong, and that we will always have men of the calibre and courage that we sent to Vietnam. Both of these groups are the lifeblood of our nation, and both can be called great. Above all I pray, as I know we all do, that men will learn to train their attitudes to respect and perceive the rights of others, so that the day finally arrives when the destruction of other human beings by war or any other means, is inconceivable.

Now, what has all of this to do with your health? — Everything. Sickness of the spirit, whether it be international, national, or local, must be dealt with first, before we can even dream about physical well-being. The "Attitudes" of men must be overhauled before there's even any **point** in pursuing physical excellence. If we live from day to day scared out of our wits because some madman has the power to blow all that we have known and loved to kingdom come, then we had better start being concerned about his *attitude,* as well as our own. The only salvation I see for man lies in his ability to change and adapt.

We have passed the point in history where military strength can guarantee us **anything.** Let's face it, and start charting a **new** course, before it's too late. We must cast aside the preposterous idea that yearning for peace somehow makes us unpatriotic or un-American. As someone has aptly stated, "I suspect that when you hear sabers rattling these days, it's because those who are wearing them are shaking in their boots." Since we cannot change the attitude of the world overnight, then we must begin slowly, by changing our own first, and then perhaps our neighbor will see those changes and his attitude will change. Goodness spreads just as easily as does evil. Maybe we can change a neighborhood, and then other neighborhoods will take notice. — All great ideas began in the mind of a man, or a group of men or women — somewhere.

Let's make another comparison to illustrate the relationship between attitude and physical health.

We have the know-how to remove a thorn from the paw of a lion, for example. In a few short days we can heal the wound and send Mr. Lion on his way to resume his activities in the jungle or forest, or wherever. But if Mr. Lion continues to hunt in the briar patch, it won't be long until he is back again with another thorn to remove. Now this can go on and on until one day he's too weak to make it back for treatment, and the jackals smell the blood and bring him down, or until he learns (change of attitude) that it's not wise to do his hunting in the briar patch. The point is — there's no sense in treating his physical wounds if we don't do something about his attitude. And so it is with all of us. We can be patched up, treated for alcoholism, have a heart by-pass, or cure our ulcers. But until we learn to stay out of the briar patch, we are only treating the **symptoms** and not the disease. If good health is really what we're after, then we have to treat the attitude first, and that starts with an honest and open look at ourselves. We must pinpoint the flaw in our attitude that is causing the distress, and then we must correct it. The key is in identifying the problem, not in treating the consequences. There are also **hidden** reasons for our attitude problems, and in an effort to understand them further I spoke at length with Ellis H. Sage, Ph.D., Consulting Psychologist for the prestigious Sansum Medical Clinic in Santa Barbara, California. Here, with his permission, are the contents of that discussion.

Dr. Sage

Question: Dr. Sage, do you feel that a person's attitude throughout their lifetime can have a direct effect upon the state of their physical health?

Answer: Yes, I do, in that the attitude of those considered is determined by several important factors. Attitude is not just the internal thinking and construction concerning the world, but also 'how the world affects the individual.' So the attitude at any specific time that you'd be viewing it would be the result of either a positive or negative stance in relationship to the issue of involvement.

Question: Then angry, combative people, for example, would view their situation from a totally different conception than, say, a docile or carefree individual, or someone who is manipulative, or frustrated, or who has recently suffered great personal loss?

Answer: You've gone through several types of personal characteristics there, and I will try to respond to a few of them. The hostile, angry person,is going to generate a lot of negative feedback from other people; therefore their hostilities and anger will likely be reinforced by the reflections of their own behavior. The chemical changes that occur in their bodies are phenominal in the scope of destructive potential. If the hostility continues over a period of time, they will in fact be destroying their bodies.

A docile individual may in reality be very emotionally responsive on the inside yet appear to be cool as a cucumber on the outside. In many cases these people are harboring a lot of negative, suppressed frustrations. On the other hand, some may just be indifferent and unable to respond either negatively or postively.

Now an individual who is manipulative is one who

doesn't have much concern for, or even care what other people feel. They can act very interested for the moment and generally make excellent first impressions. As time goes on though, other people tend to avoid getting involved with them. They are usually impulsive and irresponsible. Strangely, they seldom suffer from neurotic health problems unless they are under severe stress. When that occurs, they tend to fall apart. They are 'users of people' and rarely have any feelings of quilt, although they are great actors.

You also mentioned people who suffer great personal loss. They will often temporarily go through severe depression. A loss due to the death of a close family member or friend, the loss of an important job, we often see people who have lost three or four loved ones within the space of a few years. The departed were very important in life to those who remain, and they now find themselves totally helpless, unable to "solve the problem". That can lead to very severe depression and multiple health problems related to tension and anxiety: stomach problems, rapid heart beat, loss of appetite, etc. You can't reinstate someone who has died and the fact is that a small part of the survivor has psychologically died as well. Some people respond with anger. This can cause everything from loss of sleep to ulcers. A great many of the cases we treat for depression are caused by deep-seated anger.

Question: Doctor, you seem to stress the significance of dealing with anger; you have made it quite clear that anger is destructive and should be avoided — is there any way we can deal with this problem in our own lives?

Answer: Let's explore the other extreme. There are persons who come into my office and swear up and down that they're not angry with anyone. They will virtually never open up and express anger — they'll be smiling and pleasant, yet they will suffer back pain, neck pain, distorted sleep, tension headaches and the like, because they refuse to deal with their anger in a constructive way. They seem to prefer to deal with everyone in an angry way over dealing with the anger itself. Eventually they will have to recognize the problem and take steps to correct it if they want to put an end to the physical manifestations of it. There are ways to do it. You can't separate the individual from the attitude — so you must deal with the attitude.

Question: When people become ill or hospitalized, can their personal attitude concerning that condition really influence recovery in your opinion?

Answer: Yes, it really can. Number one, a lot of people even though they say they are open to psychological or psychiatric help, are not. They see it as a stigma. If they are willing to seek psychological help, for heaven's sake let them have it. The severely depressed need all the help they can get and we now have ways of helping these people dramatically. If they refuse to accept help or rush home from the hospital without awaiting the completion of their treatment, they're not going to get better. It's hard to know at what point an individual hurts so much that they are willing to seek help. For men in particular, it's very, very difficult. They will not admit to psychological concerns as readily as women will, and women are more willing to talk about them for the most part, therefore they get more help. Your attitude concerning the acceptance of help will play a large role in how effective that help will ultimately be.

Question: Has it been your experience, doctor, that a strong faith in one's self, or in their religion, can be a positive asset in overcoming physical or mental problems?

Answer: Yes. There are several answers to that question. If a person really believes in themselves, has confidence in themselves, they can overcome many, many things. But they must also recognize the things that are beyond their power to change. As they get older especially, they will encounter problems both physical and mental that are not as easily solved as when they were younger. They must learn to "work around" those things rather than trying to tackle them head-on as they did in their youth.

As to religion, it can be both an asset and a retardant influence. Please note that I am speaking here of "religion" — not God. It sets up social groups, it provides a context for people to interact, it defines basically some general rights and wrongs, and it gives broader meaning to our existence. The only aspect in which religion may be detrimental to health can be found in the old school of thought we used to refer to as the fundamentalists. These groups have very rigid moralistic outlooks on the human experience. They believe essentially that their religion is the answer to all problems. This leaves very little room for advancing new ideas or techniques. On some occasions lives have been lost because of the implacable stance these groups are prone to take. Psychological problems don't discriminate between a conservative, a liberal, a religious or a nonreligious person. Yet they feel that they are somehow not being a good Christian if they seek help outside of their religious sphere. It makes them very difficult to treat.

Question: Doctor Sage, I have observed that those people who survive into their 80's seem to have two things in common, rarely have I seen an exception to this. They seem to have the ability to laugh easily, and a desire to keep busy at something. Does this mean that a sense of humor and a need to be useful or productive can contribute significantly to good health or even long life?

Answer: I'm sure it's a factor. Being able to laugh is important,
            Particularly for problems that are going to
            happen in our lives no matter what, and things that
            are beyond our control that we can do nothing about.
            Yes, I think those people will survive longer. Now the
            other aspect you mentioned was having things to do.
            There is a condition I often refer to as "psychological
            senility." This is a premature withdrawal from
            reality generally found in older persons who "escape
            into the past" by reliving the significant events in their
            lives over and over again. It is brought on by the
            absence of new events to respond to, the lack of new
            problems, or challenges to deal with. Younger, more
            aggressive people will avoid them because they soon
            tire of the same old stories. Involvement in new
            interests fosters new vitality, it creates a "feedback"
            situation where their confidence is tested against the
            demands of the new project. Yes, I believe that older,
            active people are much happier, and generally feel
            much better than their inactive counterparts — my
            clinical observations confirm that.

Question: In your opinion, how can the average person deal
            with the negative aspects of a bad attitude? I should
            assume that a good starting place would be a physical
            examination for the purpose of finding any
            undiscovered health problems that may be contri-
            buting to the situation. What would you suggest on
            that, doctor?

Answer: Well, in a particular study that I made in a large
            medical clinic, all the physical factors that could
            cause psychological side effects were eliminated first.
            We focused on things which could cause them to feel
            bad: Hepatitis, mononucleosis, thyroid problems,
            or any other physical ailment, the symtoms of which
            could be mistaken for psychological problems. By
            this method we were able to zero in on those who
            could be helped from a psychological approach.

They were screened thoroughly before they ever got to me. We discovered that many people suffer from depression long before they are aware that there is a problem. Depression often comes on slowly, gradually, over long periods of time. But the symptoms can easily be mistaken for, or identified with, any number of physical ailments. Let me give you a few symptoms of depression: Fatigue, tiredness, weakness, lightheadedness, dizziness, inability to sleep well, or sleeping too long; tenseness, uneasiness, and sometimes the heart races for no apparent reason. These are things that first must be ruled out as being caused by other factors. Again, I recommend first going to a medical setting to eliminate possible physical malfuncions. Now, we get a number of patients who have gone through a goodly amount of doctors with no clarification as to their diagnosis. This usually means one of two things. Either we are not thorough enough, or the doctor is unwilling to hear that they have psychological problems.

Question: Doctor, can you personally recall any situations in your career where a change in attitude, whatever the reason for that change, brought about a marked change in someone's physical or mental health?

Answer: In terms of a patient — is that what you mean?

"Yes"

Answer: No question about it. If you can help them to finally find reasons to struggle with life, to teach them not to react to things they can do nothing about, to enjoy rewarding activities, their life can change. I might add that in this particular setting where I practice, I have access to additional help that many psychologists do not have. Today we have anti-depressants that are significant in bringing the physical body back to a physiologically nondepressed state. When you're chronically stressed for a long period of time, your body changes chemically. You can't think clearly, you can't function normally, and everything seems horrible. The new antidepressants relieve those symptoms and allow us to get back to dealing with ways in which the patient can more enjoyably experience life. It's astonishing how few people believe that they have the right to do the things they would like to do. Once they begin doing those things, they find enjoyment, fulfillment, and feel much better physically.

Question: Doctor, what about physical intake. We all know that excessive drinking or the prolonged use of drugs, for example, can alter the attitude profoundly, but how about the more common substances such as coffee, or tea, or sugar, or salt? Can these things influence personality, or mental outlook, or tolerance for stress?

Answer: They certainly can, and do. Caffeine in particular has a lot of unpleasant side effects. Over a period of time, a great many people have taught themselves that a cup of coffee will raise their spirits if they are feeling down, but the effect of caffeine is shortlived and soon they're drinking another cup, and then another. What they're doing is "hyping up," and "dropping down," which affects the blood sugar level dramatically. This in turn causes their thoughts to race,and even excels their mental function for short periods of time, yet they end up trembling, tense,anxious, unable to sleep, and are prone to overreact in stressful situations as well as under normal conditions. When they get up to 10 to 20 cups of coffee a day, they often have severe emotional problems. If they use sugar with it, they are compounding the problem. Another innocent-looking culprit in our society is the so-called "soft drink." Those who drink five or six of these popular beverages a day and "forget" to eat are subject to emotional instability. The loss of food intake further complicates the matter by inviting the physical problems associated with inadequate nourishment. Tea, if of the caffein type, must also be watched closely. Salt is a definite no-no for people with high blood pressure. These items, plus a formidable array of other everyday substances can indeed exert noticeable changes in the behavior patterns or attitude of those who ingest them in excessive amounts.

Question: Here's a tough one, doc. If you were to design a formula for the average person, with the ultimate goal being a pleasant, tolerant attitude, what suggestions would it contain?

Answer: First, I think a person has to decide what essentially in life is their goal, or goals; what directions do they want to go; what values are really important to them, and which are insignificant. I would recommend that they avoid rehearsing problems over and over in their minds, about which they can do nothing. I would urge them towards "action" regarding problems that they do possess the power to solve. When someone takes action, they alter the problem at once, because they create a feedback condition in which the problem changes shape. Even people who "stick their necks out" so to speak will be able to move forward because they are changing their environment. They are doing "something" so they don't feel helpless. The main thrust would be orientation towards action, if you want to be basically healthy. Secondly, keep an open mind to those who are in a position to help you. Whether your condition requires the services of a physician, a psychologist, or merely the sympathetic ear of a close and trusted friend, be willing to listen and evaluate.

They all see things from a position different from that of your own. Importantly, do not accept the solutions offered by any source as being totally and completely correct without weighing them against the expanded knowledge of other authoritative viewpoints.

Thirdly, realize that some of the things you have accepted as fact at some earlier point in your life may in reality be very wrong. We have all incorporated certain values into our lives, based upon earlier observations. We find ourselves re-enacting the same procedures we viewed as children at later points in our lives. We respond to conditions much in the same way as our parents did. If they dealt with their problems in a calm, analytical manner, then we shall probably do the same. If they became very emotional, or blew up and verbalized all over the place, we will more than likely react in a similar manner. What we need to do is identify the reasons for our behavior, what is causing us to be maladaptive, and what can we do about it. The solution to problems rooted in our earlier indoctrination can be found in a thorough, unimpassioned examination of "why we feel a certain way about a certain thing."

Question: Isn't that very difficult for some people, doctor?

Answer: It's very difficult for any of us, particularly if we're not totally conscious of what we're about, or what we're doing, and then if that knowledge poses a threat to us, or makes us feel insecure, it's even harder. That's essentially what counseling therapy is for. To aid individuals in finding more self-control. The more self-control you have, the more confident you will feel, and the better your attitude toward yourself and others will be.

We wish to express our gratitude to Dr. Sage
for his insightful comments.

Ignoring The Danger Signs (The R.A. Factor)

Since the beginning of time, mankind in general has chosen to ignore obvious signs of danger as they stomped across the pages of history. If not forgivable, it is at least understandable why nations, armies and other mighty contingents of solidarity, might choose to recklessly fly into the face of annihilation when they felt that their cause was just, or their purpose justified. It would be comforting to believe that national peril, the threat of subservience, or some other equally tragic imminence was always the reason behind these rash acts of men. Unfortunately this is not the case. The same disregard for danger that is so commonplace in the heroics of men locked in mortal combat under the banner of patriotism, can also be seen in the everyday choices made by a great host of our contemporaries, under far less threatening conditions. What is it, this baffling, compelling need to tempt the gods with our mindless bravado? Like moths to the flame, we are drawn to the brink of destruction time and time again by our flamboyant, cavalier scorn for anything that smacks of danger. Is it a need to flaunt our immortality? I wonder. Under certain circumstances, it must be recognized as one of the "admirable" traits which has contributed to our survival as a species. On the other hand, it can be seen as a serious flaw in our attitude, which if allowed to go unchecked, can march us inexorably in the direction of our own demise. With a minimum of consideration, we can easily see that an overabundance of the "R.A. Factor" (reckless abandon) could certainly be detrimental to our health. Why then do some of us persist? I'm convinced that it all boils down to a matter of priorities. A case of lightly weighing the possible negative aspects of some future price to be paid, against the more pleasant prospects of satisfying a current appetite or imagined need.

Let's see if that fits. By applying some simple logic against situations familiar to all of us, we should be able to determine the reasons for "R.A. Factors" and to see if they begin to conform to a certain pattern.

Why does that teenager in your family smoke? You have tried

repeatedly to get him/her to stop. You have probably made it a point to bring every new article concerning the dangers of smoking to his/her attention. You have stressed the terrible specter of serious health problems like cancer or heart disease. You have made ample remarks about their "smoker's breath" or yellowing teeth, and yet the teenager continues to smoke away as if none of these things really mattered. — That's because they don't. Not at this point in their life. What really matters to them is "how grown-up they feel," and "how well they fit into the group of peers they associate with." Those things are so much more important to them at this stage of the game than "eventual, possible health problems" that the decision isn't even close. The priority is centered in the here and now - the distant threat irrelevant.

How about the young man who chooses to work in a coal mine when he knows full well that his eventual fate will almost certainly be a case of "black lung?" Perhaps his father and his uncle are both disabled from that terrible disease, he has lived very close to the suffering, he has watched his mother struggle to support the family, and yet in spite of his superior education and ample options concerning his livelihood, he returns to the ground as did all of the other real "men" in his memory. — His priority is his manhood. And he interprets this to mean that he must pit his youth and strength against the monster which felled his father. The possible health results will not dissuade him from that challenge.

The same is true of other "high-risk" employment. If your whole family has been trapeze artists, you may feel that you "must" continue in this tradition in spite of the strong flashes of reason which urge you toward a safer occupation and the prospects of a longer, happier life.

The "R.A. Factor" is present to some degree in all of our lives. Why does a happily married man with a great family decide to "risk" all that he has by running around with other women? - Priorities. Perhaps he has a need to prove that he's still "got it" to himself or to some of his friends. Why does a young mother with children to raise and a fine husband at home, "gamble" with all of their future lives by "jaywalking" in the middle of the block when she could easily walk a few steps more and avoid the terrible risk? - Priorities. Maybe she's fearful that someone will snatch up that cute little dress that's on sale across the street.

Why will an otherwise stable person take their life savings and "blow" it all on the crap tables or the race track? They know the risk and they are mindful of the odds of losing, yet they do it anyway. Why? I for one do not believe that "the lure of winning all that money" is the real reason. I am persuaded instead that this person has a high "R.A. Factor" and is, in fact, feeding another immediate need which has taken priority over the possible destructive outcome of losing all that they own. It's quite conceivable that after a great many years of scrimping and saving, they find it highly exhilerating to "throw all caution to the winds" and "go for broke" without heeding the nagging shackels of restraint that have dominated their every move for all those years past.

Now, if we review the aforementioned examples, we will almost certainly arrive at two conclusions. One: That if these people had really stopped to think about the possible consequences of their actions, they would have chosen instead to avoid the danger; and two: That satisfying an immediate priority at the risk of life, limb, health, or prosperity is only practiced by those individuals who have not as yet learned the difference between bravery and foolishness. How I wish that were the case. Unfortunately, it is not. That strange attraction for the forbidden; that need to test our bounderies and defy our restrictions, no mattter the cost, has been with us since the Garden of Eden. It has been at once a blessing and a curse. It has been instrumental in countless breakthroughs in science, technology, industrialization, social upheaval, and many other courageous attempts to right the wrongs of humanity. Simultaneously, it has on too many occasions spawned attempts by the disciples of power to ruthlessly seize whatever they would aspire to, indiscriminately crushing all opposition in their path with utter disregard for the legitimate rights of others. So the need arises to "identify" this ingredient in our attitudes which so powerfully influences what manner of man or woman we shall become.

I want you to consider with me the full implications of the "R.A. Factor," "R.A." being an abbreviation for the term "reckless abandon." Let's first examine closely the full meaning of that expression. "Reckless," according to my ancient dictionary, is described thusly:

> "Utterly careless of the consequences of action:
> Without caution."

"Abandon" is elaborated upon somewhat, but for our purposes here, it is described in this fashion:

> "To give up all concern, to give up all control,
> to forsake utterly."

Not a very good ingredient to have as part of one's attitude. Realization that it is present to some degree in the attitude of each of us may be the first step in learning to control it. The potential for self-destruction in this ingredient should be starkly apparent to all of us, and the threat to our physical health and longevity certainly requires no explanation.

If we look for a moment at the actions of those people who have a very high "R.A. Factor," we can easily see that the probability of a short life span rises in relationship to the factor. Bear in mind the two elements present in the "R.A. Factor" — "A" A need to satisfy some immediate priority, and "B" A strange attraction for danger or risk. A classic example would be that of a young man showing off his automobile. He can be seen dodging in and out of traffic in an attempt to be noticed. He wants the whole world to know that he has arrived on the scene of licensed, "grownup" drivers, and that he has a beautiful car with which to enter that "questionable" arena. As he approaches a blind curve at the top of a hill, he decides to pass the car in front of him, seemingly oblivious to the fact that if another car happens to be coming from the other direction, there is almost no possible chance that he will survive the encounter. How about the innocent family that might be in the oncoming car? Has he thought about them? Yes, — he gave them a minimal thought, but then a strong, present priority took control of his decision, and he silently laughed in the face of danger and pressed the gas pedal to the floor. —

What was that priority? Was it a need to prove to himself that he had courage? Was he determinded to prove that his car was superior to that Cadillac in front of him? — I hope he made it.

Another example might be the person who has been suffering chest pains, but flatly refuses to see a doctor. He knows very well that he is treading on dangerous ground and what the possible results might be, but he has another priority. He has portrayed himself to his family over the years as "the indestructible man." Never let sickness stop him from going to work, never cried when he was hurt. Now he will defy the dangers that threaten him, even though his life may be forfeit. The "R.A. Factor" can be a killer. Let's recognize it in our own lives, so that we may "control" it. Abiding threats to our lives must be labeled foolishness in the extreme. Let's avoid it.

Now how about you? In what manner and to what degree has the "R.A. Factor" infiltrated your attitude? Here are some areas you might investigate.

> Do you always pick up the whole check when you dine with friends — even though you know the rent is overdue, or some other important bill has to be paid?
> Could your priority be "big-shotitis?"

> Do you drive a car that is really too expensive for your income, while your family has to do without dental care, or some other important necessity?
> Could your priority be "the image you present?"

> Do you have some of the seven danger signals of cancer, but laugh them off because you're "too mean to die?"
> Could your priority be a "superman image?"

> Do you take large risks in your business ventures and

> then "worry" about them for weeks afterwards?
> Could your priority be that of of a "wheeler-dealer?"
>
> Do you drink to excess, or "do" drugs when you
> know that sooner or later you will pay with your
> health or your life?
> Could you be defying the danger, or trying to escape
> something in the present?

Please understand that this list is not meant to be an indictment of anyone nor is it meant to point an accusing finger. It is meant only to outline to some extent the hidden ways in which the "R.A. Factor" can stealthily rob us of our values, our health, or worse.

It is hoped that an awareness of the "R.A. Factor" would cause each of us to examine more closely the reasons for some of our actions,and at the same time to look for these symptoms in the attitude of others. It is doubtful that you would want your business partner, stock broker, banker, doctor or lawyer to be a person with a high "R.A. Factor." — Think about it.

I must conclude this section with an important observation which may at first glance appear to be in conflict with some of the things I said earlier. I **do** believe in taking chances, in reaching for the moon, in being the very best that you can be, in stretching in order to grow. But I do **not** believe in gambling that which you cannot afford to lose, nor in risking the priceless possessions that are given to you only once, such as your health, your life, your family, etc. These things you do not intentionally gamble with, and you certainly do not risk losing them because of a frivolous "priority" which doesn't even compare to them in true value. Perhaps the real lesson to be learned here is "knowing the difference between the two."

The Rebellious Kite

When my children were small, I used to tell them the story of the rebellious kite. I believe it may be worth the retelling at this point in our chat, as the subject we are about to discuss is especially pertinent to the younger generation who will be "making their way" in the years that lie ahead. Oldsters will also recognize the traits of many of their past and present friends in this section, with the added advantage of having seen the results of the "attitudes" we are about to investigate.

There was once a young boy who was given a large and beautiful kite for his birthday. He was extremely proud of the new possession, and he flew it as often as he possibly could, until his skill with the kite became known far and wide. By carefully trimming and resetting the tail and the crossbeams, he was able to masterfully coax the kite to heights far greater than anyone had ever seen a kite flown before. Day after day he would gently maneuver the beautiful kite upward and outward before the summer breeze until it was no more than a tiny speck in the sky to those who were watching. As the boy slowly and carefully raised the kite to ever greater heights, the fame of its astonishing performance spread to many distant places. People would gather in great crowds to cheer and applaud as the famous kite was "ever so carefully" brought back to earth at the end of the day. As time went on, the mighty kite began to look forward to the applause and the cheers of the admiring throng. It also began to resent the restraints placed upon it by its young master. Slowly at first, the kite began to buck and dive and zig-zag crazily in the spacious blue sky. It became harder and harder to control as the days passed, and finally one day it decided to pull away from the restrictive string that held it firmly rooted to the young boy below. It sought the strong winds which seemed to whisper "Come with me, we will fly beyond the great mountains, I will show you places that you have never seen, you no longer need the boy." With a mighty tug, the great kite snapped the string that held it. For a brief time it flew high and free, almost forgetting the small young boy who had lovingly nurtured it to fame and admiration. But then it realized quite suddenly that something it needed badly was missing. The wind which had promised so much was now laughing heartlessly as the once famous kite spun dizzily towards the earth below, out of control, and at the mercy of every crazy rush of air which chose to make sport of its helpless, now tragic condition. When the kite finally crumpled to the ground, it lay there quietly watching the great birds of the air soaring majestically through the heavens as it had so often done. Soon the young boy was kneeling beside it on the ground, speaking softly, tearfully to his fallen friend. "Oh kite, my beautiful kite, why did you try so hard to break away from my help? I only wanted you to be the greatest kite in the world." The kite replied slowly, sadly, and with the knowledge that often comes with tragic mistakes, "I never realized that the same thing which held me back — held me up."

Most of us have at one time or another been very much like the kite in this child's tale, resenting every step of the way the boundaries of love that have been set for us by those who really care. Our inclination is to discard as "old-fashioned" the constructive criticism given us by that small, select group of people in our lives who have nothing to gain except the pleasure of seeing us do well. These few people should in reality be our "golden circle" of advisors. Some of the ancient voices may "crack" slightly when speaking, or be weak or slow in forming words, but they come from the heart, and that my friend is hard to find.

I suppose it's only fair to acknowledge that "it is the way of life" for the new generations to "break away" and to "break new ground" and I say thank God for that, but "breaking the string" so gently held by the hands that have lifted us aloft is tantamount to denying a portion of our own being. We need the love of the faithful few, and they need our love as well. When our children reach the age of 16 or perhaps 17, they oftentimes view this remarkable achievement as though they had reached the age of "total knowledge." This is certainly not news to those of you who have raised a family. The conflict between "I'm old enough to do so and so - Sally's mother lets her," and "I don't want you doing so and so" is practically an everyday occurrence. The bright spot in this so-called "generation gap" is the subtle merging of opposing viewpoints. Its purpose is twofold:

One: It prepares the child for adulthood.

Two: It prepares the parent for "letting go."

The child in question soon learns that Mom or Dad knew what they were talking about, and the parent learns that their "baby" has grown up. There is, however, a danger which lurks within this transition stage from child to young adult. The severity of this danger will vary according to the *attitude* of the person involved and has to do with the *"interpretation"* of the attainment of newfound freedoms. Some will inevitably consider each new step in the direction of their personal freedoms, as a signal to abandon all previously learned guidelines. Although we all go through a certain amount of "bridge burning" upon our "release" from childhood, most of us return by degrees both large and small to the values of our teachers. Life has a way of "socking it to us" when we ignore the disciplines and responsibilities which must be a part of the well-rounded attitude.

Regrettably true, however, is the fact that a great many people who have been exposed to the "heady stuff" of personal freedom before they were ready, never again return to the disciplines of knowledge, character, or the ability to "govern" their actions to harmonize with the symphony of "mutual regard" so necessary to a pleasant excursion through our appointed time frame.

The real damage occurs almost as an aftershock. Once the mind has determined to resent and resist all previous boundaries, it's practically a "knee-jerk" action to forcefully prohibit the influx of any "new" limits - or knowledge. The curse that accompanies this posture is *stagnation*.

The bearers of this affection are easily recognized. Theirs is a life of "hot frustration." They are the loudest defenders of their points of view and will argue stubbornly on, even though facts to the contrary are overwhelming. They are the first to condemn and the last to congratulate. When offered advice, they will "attack" the validity of that advice, and often verbally belittle the person giving it. Their plans fall apart on every front, but they always have "other people to blame" for their failures. They are extremely self-centered and show very little interest in the achievements of others. They will talk all night about themselves or "hold court" so long as they are the center of attention, but if someone else is in the limelight, they will excuse themselves in a gesture of disinterest or disappear altogether.

Now what have we to gain by looking so closely at the imperfections of someone like this? Well, I don't think there's a one of us who hasn't encountered someone very similar during our lifetime, at least once. We know what the results of this manner of lifestyle are, we have seen them. The inabilitiy to hold a job, the constant loss of friends, the endless striving for recognition. What a horrible way to live. So what exactly can we do to avoid winding up with an attitude like that?

The answer is not a short one. To begin with, I think we have to recognize that "The day we stop learning from others is the day we stop learning." Secondly, we must establish in our own minds, once and for all, the inescapable reality that our attitudes are the "prime movers" of, and inseparably linked to, the forces that control our health, prosperity, and general well-being. A little thought on the subject will quickly expose the relationship between bad health and bad attitude, for example. The person who has deliberately declined the "helping hands" of knowledgeable friends because of a misplaced ego which refuses to admit that "Someone may just possibly know something that they don't," is "in effect" stifling their own chance at growth. The failure to reach financial security as a case in point, can easily contribute to a detrimental health situation. High blood pressure, ulcers, stress and many other physical problems could most certainly be alleviated if the afflicted party wasn't worried sick about how they were going to make the mortgage payment next month. The quality of life is drastically affected, make no mistake, by the end results produced by our attitudes.

If you will assist me in a little conjecture, perhaps I can illustrate the vast differences in the quality of life between two men traveling the same road whose "attitudes" have brought them to enormously divergent perceptions of the same set of circumstances.

John Gibbons:

John Gibbons was feeling rather proud of himself. It had taken a lot of years of hard work, but now at last he knew that it had all been worth it. As he sped across the desert in his air conditioned Cadillac, his thoughts drifted back to that day in New York when the three top bosses had asked him to step into the office for a few minutes. He smiled to himself as he remembered the uncomfortable little knot that had mysteriously grown inside his stomach. He remembered thinking "Ow, that hurts," as he rapped his knuckles firmly against the huge oak door. "Come in," a strong clipped voice had commanded. That would be Mr. Grey, the vice president. As he had pushed aside the massive door, he found himself confronted by the full attention of the three men. Mr. Grey's piercing blue eyes had lacered directly to his own. "Come in John, have a seat over here. Would you like a drink?" John had gracefully declined and settled himself comfortably into one of the overstuffed tan suede chairs at the front of Mr. Grey's desk. With almost no hesitation, Mr. Grey had begun to speak. "John, you've been with us for eighteen years now, isn't that right?" "Yes, it'll be nineteen in October." "How would you feel about making a little change?" "Well, what kind of change?" "We're opening a new office in Los Angeles. As a matter of fact we've already opened it, and we all agree that you would be the man that we would like to see head it up." John had been momentarily stunned. As he had recovered from the jolt, he had smiled directly at Mr. Grey and said, "Did you say a 'little' change?" "Well, maybe not so little," he had replied. "John, you're a good man, and you know the business. I'd rest a lot easier if I knew there was someone like you 'cracking the whip' out there. Now I don't want you to make up your mind right this minute. Go home, talk to your wife and let me know by the end of the week - is that time enough?" John had caught the "get-things-done" spirit that always seemed to bubble out of Mr. Grey, and he had replied without really thinking about any possible complications, "I'll make it enough time." "Good boy," Mr. Grey had said, "Let me know as soon as you decide. There will of course be a substantial raise in pay for you." He had left the office feeling a bit light headed, like the first time he had ridden the roller coaster. He knew from past experience that if Mr. Grey said "a substantial raise," he **meant** a substantial raise. After the decision to take the position had been made, there followed a month of madness. Selling the old house where the children had been raised, deciding what to take and what to get rid of, flying to Los Angeles to find a new place to live, all of these things plus countless other details had to be dealt with. Now those necessary chores were behind him. His wife was comfortably settled in their new California home and he was at this moment driving out to join her to begin their new life. He mused silently to himself, "Boy, you just never know, who would have thought at this time last year that I would be heading for California to start over again. Well, maybe that's not quite true. Actually, I'll just be continuing on in my chosen profession, at higher pay, in a better location, with a challenge that I'm really going to enjoy." He paused momentarily in his mental assessments. "God, I love it," he grinned. He flicked the stereo on and was bountifully blessed with a medly of old "Leroy Anderson, Mantovani" melodies. As he floated easily down the long desert highway, his mind seemed to focus in on the beauty that was all about him. He watched with amusement as the desert breezes playfully created dancing little whirlwinds to get his attention. Like children trying to be noticed, they valiantly stirred up as much of a ruckus as they could, and would occasionally "whoosh" across the highway in a great show of feigned ferocity.

The purple mountains in the distance seemed also to be competing for his approval. They managed the light and the shadows expertly to create their own stark beauty against the clear, light blue desert sky. John had yielded to the "overtures to be appreciated" that this vast land was singing to him, and had eased the great car slowly to a halt at a wide space on the road. As he had alighted and bounded atop a huge flat rock to better view his surroundings, he was at once rewarded with the sweet desert smell of sagebrush and flowers. The countless, colorful little desert flowers were all nodding their approval for as far as the eye could see. Even the cactus plants which were scattered about like ever-vigilant sentries seemed to be preening themselves in the warmth of the sun. John shielded his eyes and gazed far off down the slim, naked highway so carelessly guarded by the unruly fenceposts which had succumbed to the carefree ways of the desert. He thought of his future. He thought also of the many sacrifices that he and his wife had made to get to this point. How they had postponed many of their own dreams through the years in order to better prepare the children for the lives that they would lead. He remembered with some pride how he and his wife Helen had decided to "put off" that long dreamed-of trip to Hawaii so their son Joe could enter college.

Dear Helen. Her support over the years could only be described as incredible. Her willingness to forgo her own pleasures and dreams so that he and the children could pursue goals important to them was priceless. "Now it's Helen's turn," he thought. "I'm going to make up for all the things she's done without, and I'm going to start enjoying life myself. I've had to swallow my pride more than once to accomodate inconsiderate clients. Now our time has come."

It was strange how close he suddenly felt to the natural beauty that was all around him. Almost as though he had become a part of it all. He somehow felt akin to good, and beauty, and life, and truth. He pondered the strange feeling for some time, and then concluded that he had in fact arrived at a "oneness" with life. He could gaze backward without regret to the difficult challenges he had met in life, and he could savor those decisions that had been made for the best interest of people he loved. The price he had paid in personal toil and financial setback now seemed to be jewels in his crown of achievement. The doubts he had experienced about moving to California had disappeared into the vastness of life so evident from his vantage point atop the desert rock. He smiled and nodded back at the desert flowers. He knew now that it would be alright, that this was a beginning, that a new chapter in his life was about to unfold. As he walked slowly back to the car, his hair was playfully rumpled about his head as his new friend, the desert wind, said goodbye.

Jay Banning:

The old Chevy lumbered laboriously across the hot, windy desert. Jay had fixed his gaze on the intermittent white lines that separated the lanes of highway. One after another they slipped into view, glaring briefly in the hot sun and then disappearing until the next replacement arrived. He let his eyes shift slowly to the endless line of telephone poles which paralleled the highway for as far as he could see. "There must be a billion of those damn things between here and Los Angeles." he thought. "I pity the poor idiots who had to put them all up in this hell hole. It must have taken them years." The smell of hot motor oil was in his nostrils. Not quite strong enough to make him cough, but sufficient to cause a slight sting in his lungs and to add to the uncomfortable boredom he felt for the whole trip. "What the hell am I doing here," he thought. "I probably never should have left New York. If it wasn't for that stupid boss of mine I'd still be back there." His mind drifted back to the events that had fallen together like a "stacked deck" to ultimately strip him of alternatives and force him to "do something desperate" or get sucked under by "that whole rotten bunch" of leeches that his ex-wife hung around with. Wilma had been a pretty good wife he thought. Until she had met Gloria, the boss's wife. After that it was argue, argue all the damn time. "I don't know what ever got into that woman, she just never seemed to realize that money doesn't grow on trees. Sure, Gloria could throw it around like confetti, her old man had been foreman for sixteen years, but a poor working stiff like me just don't have that kinda' bread to blow. For years Wilma had understood how it is with a guy like me. She never complained about my Saturday nights and she just took it for granted that I was gonna get drunk and try to relax one lousy day out of the week. Nope, Gloria ruined her, and the two kids have to suffer now because that dame thought she knew what was best for Wilma." Jay reached for another beer from the styrofoam container. A strong gust of wind hit the small car broadside and jolted Jay into full concentration and a strong grip on the steering wheel with his left hand. "Damn desert," he thought. He held the cold beer against his hot sweaty face for a moment. It felt refreshing, a reminder that there were cool things somewhere in this world, but not here, not in this damn hot box. He took a long, slow swallow. How long had it been since the divorce? Three years? No, almost four years now. God, time gets away from you. "The kids must be six and eight now. I'm glad I never went to see them, it would just make it harder on me." He took another swallow and started thinking about the last two months. "I guess all this crap started just because I was a few months late with the child support payments. Hell, I've got a right to live too." Old Charlie, the boss, had called him into the little tarpaper shack that served as an office at the construction sites and asked him to "have a seat" on one of the dusty wooden chairs. "Jay," he had said. "We've got a problem. Wilma's lawyers have put an attachment against your checks for back child support." "WHAT! How the hell can they do that?" "They can do it, and I have to send your checks directly to the court. I can't pay you, Jay." "**Are you serious?** Just what the hell do you expect me to live on?" "It's a court order, Jay. If I don't comply with it, they'll have **me** up before the judge." Jay had answered hotly, his eyes reflecting his rage. "Well, if you think I'm gonna bust my butt around here for nothin', you've got another 'think' comin'."

Old Charlie had tried to remain calm. His voice was low but firm as he spoke. "Jay, there's only one thing to do. Get together with Wilma and her attorneys and see if you can't work something out. I know she's having a tough time of it. She was over at the house crying the other day because she hasn't got the money to pay the rent." "Well, that's just tough, she got what she wanted, she should have thought about that before she filed for divorce." Charlie was losing his patience. He looked Jay full in the eye and laid it out straight. "Look Jay, you've got two beautiful kids there and a fine woman who are trying their best to get by. Now why don't you try to straighten this thing out before it gets out of hand. If you don't, the cops are going to pick you up sure as hell, and then where will you be?" Jay was in no mood to be agreeable, his Tennessee accent was always prominent when he was angry. He used to kid about it in pleasanter times, "It's funny, but I sound just like my old man when I get mad," he had said. On this occasion he was "Daddy" all over again. He spoke slowly and threateningly. "Sure Charlie, take Wilma's side, everybody does, but I'll tell you something. I'm not gonna spend any time in jail, and I'm sure as hell not gonna call that woman and apologize for running out of money." He turned to leave and "spat" sarcastically over his shoulder, "Good-bye Charlie, thanks for nothin'." As Jay reflected on the events of that last day in New York, he couldn't help being a little amazed at the speed with which all of this had taken place. He had gone directly from the job site to his small room about four miles away, threw his few belongings into a couple of pillow cases, tossed them into the car, and headed for the road to California.

That first night he had driven right straight through, without stopping to rest. About six o'clock the next evening it had begun to catch up with him. He had wheeled the old car into a motel which had "cheap" written all over it. As he turned the engine off, he was vaguely aware that his wrists hurt him from the many miles of gripping the steering wheel in prolonged anger. He was tired, dead tired, and the promise of a hot cup of coffee, a bite to eat, and a nice clean bed seemed to surpass in importance, all of the reasons he had for being there. The following morning he had awakened to the busy whine of truck tires singing their song of distant places where they were bound. He silently cursed the lateness of the hour as he squinted through sleep-dimmed eyes at the old silver-colored wrist watch. He wolfed down his bacon and eggs and hot coffee, threw a "quarter" tip on the counter and hurriedly paid the bill at the nearby truck stop. Outside at the gas pump he listened with annoyance to the ding-ding-ding of the "dated" machine as it ticked away the gallons and the dollars needed to put distance between him and his problems in New York. The station attendant spoke politely, "Nice mornin'." Jay mustered a less than enthusiastic "Yeah." After a few more "dings" from the gas pump the attendant spoke again. "Hey mister, you better do something about this right front tire if you plan to drive very far. I can see the cord showing through in one spot. Jay lied convincingly in spite of the unpleasant news, "Yeah, I'm keeping an eye on it." "Damn," he thought, "what next."

The next two days had brought him through the mountainous areas of the East, and through the long boring corn and wheat fields of the Mid-West. Now he had this endless desert to cross and then a few more mountains in the West before reaching Los Angeles and — whatever awaited him there. His thoughts were interrupted by the bump-bump-bump of the right front tire. He guided the old Chevy cautiously to a sandy spot at the side of the road. As he slammed the squeaky door and walked around the front of the car, he could hear the unmistakeable "hissss" of a radiator pleading for water.

The tire looked bad. A huge knot had formed at the "bare" spot and it was plainly apparent that a few more miles of revolutions would be the most he could expect. He jerked open the trunk of the old car and wrestled the spare out onto the sand where he could look it over. He squinted his eyes protectively against the sharp little bursts of wind and sand that stung his face repeately. The spare was fully inflated, thank God, but the tread had disappeared in several spots, and he knew that it would be "stretching it" to get all the way to Los Angeles on this poor excuse for a tire. Nevertheless, he went through the ancient ritual of replacing the right front tire by means of the complicated bumper jack, which he was sure had been designed for the express purpose of "frustrating" those who would one day have to use it. He then raised the hood of the car, fetched the styrofoam container in which the ice had melted, and gingerly poured the contents into the radiator.

As he completed these tasks, a wave of despondency overcame him. He walked slowly to the great flat rock which was nearby and climbed atop it to view his surroundings. Fear for the future seemed to engulf him from out of nowhere. As he gazed out upon the vast desert, he wondered how many men had perished in pursuit of their dreams on this relentless, pitiless land of sorrows. Within sight of his gaze he saw only signs of destruction. The remains of old wooden buildings lay crumpled in the sand far in the distance. The fenceposts along the highway had long since lost their usefulness and were now only decaying monuments to the futility of man. What would his life be like in Los Angeles? Would he end up battered and broken and of no use to anyone, like the fenceposts? Or would he at last find a life of happiness, of usefulness and someone to love. "Well," he thought. "I won't find out standing on this damn rock." He climbed into the old Chevy and started the engine. He eased her onto the highway and built her speed gradually through the gears. A desert hawk perched serenely atop a telephone pole watched quizzically as the old Chevy grew smaller and smaller and finally disappeared completely into the distant, "waterlike" heat waves of the great desert.

Looking Back — For The Future

Alright, let's first dispense with the obvious assumptions that many readers may make when comparing the lives of these two men. We know that they are traveling the very same geographical road, and that they are theoretically about to begin new lives in a different location. But there the similarity ends. The roads that each of these men have chosen are as unalike as night and day, not because there is any appreciable difference in what they see, but because "the way that they see it" sets them apart as distantly as the North and South Poles. We can see a little bit of ourselves in the "attitudes" of both of these men. Essentially, we all travel the same road, but our interpretation of what we see, our "attitudes" will make the journey one of pleasant and good surroundings, or of ominous and frightening dangers. The thing that we don't seem to have realized thus far is the terribly important reality that it is "we" who will ultimately have to live in the world we have created for ourselves by the chain reaction, cause and effect, or power of retribution that functions as the result of our attitudes.

We view situations like Jay Banning's with a focus on the material differences between what the two men possess. "Sure it's hard for Jay to be optimistic, he's driving a beat up old Chevy while John Gibbons is cruising down the highway in an air conditioned Cadillac." Our attention should be focused on the **reasons** for this. The world is filled with people who are experts at justifying failure. **Why** is one man heading happily towards a new life while the other is "running scared" from the old one? I don't think we can really understand that, unless we look "backward" to see how the attitude of each has influenced his life. Let's assume that both men are the same age, both come from middle class families, and both have had equal opportunities for education. From the little we know about each of them, we can spot sizable differences in attitude. John spent both his time and his money trying to prepare his children for a life of their own. Jay, on the other hand, married much later in life and was concerned only about "his" feelings after the divorce. John stuck it out at a job that wasn't always too pleasant, and earned the respect of his bosses in the process. Jay "blamed" his boss for many of his problems, and wound up leaving his job. John is a man who gave much of himself to family. Jay could "care less" about what happens to them. The irony here is that the man who "gave the most" ended up with the most. And that rule of life hasn't changed since God first put us here.

Now, if this short portion of their life stories is any indication of how they have behaved in the past, it doesn't take a genius to figure why one is on the road to success and the other is on the road to—more of the same.

If we had known them both from birth, we probably could have seen the handwriting on the wall. John may have worked his way through college while Jay dropped out of school to earn "big money" in construction. As each of these men came to forks in the road of life, the factor which influenced their decisions more than any other—and you can bet on it—was their attitude.

If we "project" now, even with the scanty information we have here, we can almost predict what their lives will be like in the future. There is one hopeful note regarding our friend "Jay" though. Some men and women have changed the course of their lives profoundly—by a change in attitude. More on that later in the book.

A final comment on these two men. Which of the two do you think would be inclined towards better health? One carries the memory of a job well done with his family. The other carries the guilt of a job undone with his children. One has established himself in the business world. The other is still trying to get organized.

I will again quote Catherine Houck in her excellent article in Reader's Digest:

> *"Evidence is building that suggests emotions play an important part in virtually **all** illness."*

CHAPTER SIX

ATTITUDE AND SUCCESS

Oh Lordy!! The volumes that have been written about success, especially in the last fifteen years or so. It seems that every time someone lucks into a few bucks, they become prime candidates to write a book expounding their "sure-fire" methods for accumulating vast riches overnight. I have often wondered what it would be like to read an "honest-to-God" account of some of these success stories with the unwritten facts filled in for us. They would probably sound something like this:

"I had been pinching pennies for years until I discovered the 'fat-cat' system for making money. Now I'm no genius, but the secret formula I discovered while picking strawberries on my day off has made me a very wealthy man. There was an old house in our town which had always fascinated me as a boy. I remember thinking many times 'Gee, with a little paint and some fixing up that old place would be worth a lot of money.'

I began to spend my weekends painting and repairing the house—because it was far better than picking strawberries. (In the meantime my aunt Martha died leaving me fifty 'big ones.') By watching my money carefully (and teaching my scout troup that 'painting can be fun,') I was able to restore the great old house to its former grandeur. With some reluctance I hung the 'For Sale' sign on the front porch, and waited anxiously for someone to call. (Unfortunately, nobody was interested.) Imagine my surprise when a few months later (twenty-six to be exact,) a developer approached me and said they were planning a shopping center in that area, and would I be interested in selling the old place. (Dumb luck there.) My heart pounded as he wrote out a check for twice the amount I had paid for it. The old showplace had again become a thing of beauty, enchanting all who chanced to see her. (The developer promptly tore it down and put up a fish market.) I had discovered the road to riches quite by accident, and I knew that I had to share my good fortune with all of the poor people out there. That's why I'm making you this special offer. Just send me ten dollars, and I'll teach you the magic formula for becoming rich overnight. (It it doesn't work — what the hell.)"

We are poking fun here of course, but the fact remains that many who propose to show you easy steps to wealth, are in reality far more interested in lining their own pockets at your expense. I do not mean to imply that we cannot learn from others. Clearly our discussion in the previous chapter should have established my feelings concerning that subject, but we need to "think beyond surface appearances" and discard as readily as we would soiled clothing, the tempting proposition that we can purchase our success at bargain rates.

I don't think we can effectively evaluate the relationship between our attitudes and success without first establishing to some degree, or at least "defining" to some degree, the meaning of the word *"success."*

We know at once, that it means different things to different people. My interpretation of success may be entirely contrary in content, to yours. So "success" then becomes a personal thing, based upon the achievement of "personal" goals, ambitions, or dreams.

We tend to oversimplify the meaning of success in our society and assume that anyone displaying the outward appearances of financial stability is by reason of the "things" he or she possesses, a success. The truth is — and this may be hard to believe for some — there are countless numbers of wealthy people in this world who would trade every dime of their financial possessions if they could only regain something of greater value which they once had and somehow lost along the way.

The ability to "buy" things is of no value whatsoever if your health is such that you cannot enjoy a moment of peace without pain.

A stunning mansion, stocked with fine thoroughbred horses, a collection of the world's most admired automobiles, and decorated with famous paintings, becomes nothing more than a museum for envious onlookers if there are not people around whom you love, and who love you, to share it with. So success in any form is a hollow victory unless you have provided for "the sharing of love" as an absolutely fundamental necessity to ensure your own happiness and fulfillment.

I have known many extremely wealthy people who were *failures* at life. And I have been privileged to know hundreds of "average" appearing people who quietly and selflessly chose to provide for the "greater good" of someone other than themselves as their personal goal of success. I admire these people unreservedly. As an unobserved onlooker, I have been thrilled many times by watching their reactions as the recipient of their love achieved his or her goal, thereby attaining for the "givers" success. These people never share in the limelight, nor are there any fanfares for their selflessness. But the act of watching them quietly wipe the tears of joy from their eyes as their loved ones attain recognition or successful goals, is an experience far more moving than that of observing the ribbon cutting ceremonies as a wealthy man opens yet another multimillion dollar skyscraper, dedicated in reality to the pursuit of more dollars. So once again we can see that the truly great rewards of this life are to be found not in the course of amassing personal fortunes, but rather in the little acts of pure love that warm forever the hearts of both the giver and the receiver.

Smilin' Billy

My wife and I had taken the little log cabin in the Sierras under the pretext of looking for a quiet place where we could get away from the business and social pressures of Santa Barbara long enough to concentrate on other values, and perhaps to allow myself a little freedom of thought in the completion of a book I was writing.

The truth was, we loved it up there, and we couldn't wait to smell the pine forests again and to lie quietly on the banks of soft pine needles above Lake Mary, soaking up the warm friendly rays of clear mountain sunlight that seemed to penetrate to the soul, and to recharge energies as surely as did the legendary fountain of youth.

Secretly, I knew that the screeching of a busy bluejay could be just as distracting as was the unwelcome jangling of a nervous telephone, which seemed bent upon destroying all nerve centers. Nevertheless, our love for the High Sierra prevailed, and soon we were moved into our mountain hideaway, busily shoving pots and pans, boxes, and assorted other so-called essentials into their respective niches. I have never been able to figure out why my sweet wife, who is otherwise a master planner, always manages to "forget" that I have to put my typewriter — somewhere. Maybe it's in retaliation for that time I made her put her sketches out on the back porch. Hell hath no fury like an "artist" scorned. Anyhow, she finally decided to "give the kid a break" and allowed me to set up the battered old typewriter on the kitchen table where I could gaze "thoughtfully" out of the window towards shimmering Lake Mary. Readjusting to a comfortable schedule went rather smoothly, and within a day or two we had developed a routine whereby I could "peck away" for a few hours in the mornings and then we could have the balance of the day to explore, revel in the beauty around us, and otherwise enjoy one another's company.

I loved those days together. Our children were pretty well grown up by then (we had seven,) and it was oddly like getting acquainted all over again during those moments of our life when we were alone — together. I had somehow forgotten over the years when she was "Mommy" and I was "Daddy" what great company she really was. She could be cute, witty and mischevious, and I silently scolded myself for not realizing in the years that had passed, how deeply she loved the things of the forest. She took the greatest delight in watching a ground squirrel scramble for acorns, and she would often jerk me to a halt just so she could stop and examine a wildflower closely. Our evenings were spent on the back porch above the lake, listening to the night sounds, or I would sit alone as I listened to her singing along with the radio as she prepared the evening meal. There was something indescribably comforting about the concert of her voice, above the music, intermingled with the sounds of crickets, an occasional owl or lake frog, and the sizzle of something delicious frying in the pan. The aroma of fried potatoes and pork chops, when mixed with the clear, pine-scented mountain air, is enough to awaken the appetite of a marble statue. Following the evening meal, we would dim the lights and retire to the old porch where we would strain our imaginations in an effort to identify the numerous strange noises that drifted up to our cabin from the vicinity of the lake. It was a pleasant way to conclude the day.

Mornings were something else altogether. They usually began with the clackety-clack of my old typewriter, followed closely by a moan from the bedroom; then, after a brief moment of silence, a short conversation that never did vary much in content from the following account:

Jackie: Honey, do you have to "clack" that thing so loudly in the mornings? I'm trying to sleep.

Rog: Honey, it's an electric typewriter. No matter how softly I touch the keys, it's still going to "clack". Even if I type with gloves on it's going to "clack". If I barely, barely, barely touch the keys — you got it — "clack." Now why don't you get up and make us some coffee?

Jackie: Oh all right, I can't sleep anyhow (mumble, mumble, mutter, mutter.)

After our morning cups of coffee we would usually step outside to watch the forest come to life. It was quite a sight really. The sun would knife through the trees in long, brilliant rays of light, the animals and birds would be rushing in all directions as if they had a million things to do before nightfall, and even the fish in Lake Mary could be heard flopping loudly against the surface of the water as if to say "Hey guys, don't forget us, we're here too."

The morning walks were the best part, though. It had become part of our daily ritual to walk hand in hand down to the little settlement which served as the supply center for everyone who lived near the lake. These morning walks will always stand out in my memory as one of my life's most pleasant experiences. It was only about a mile and a half to the settlement, but the laughter my wife and I shared on those short journeys, the comraderie, and the feeling of nature experienced at its beautiful best, cannot accurately be described in the confines of the printed page. We would crunch over the dead pine needles, at times kicking up little clouds of forest dust that created beautiful gold-flecked patterns in the "stab-like" rays of sunshine which chopped their way through the tall pine forest. Always in the distance were the snow-crowned Sierra Nevada, their rugged blue-grey austerity overseeing the antics of the forest children like doting grandparents. At one point we would walk along the lake for about half a mile. On those mornings we could smell the freshness and cleanness of the lake as her many animal residents hustled about their business in a great show of "important purpose." We could smell the fullness of life in the mud banks along the lake, and we laughed together at the "snooty" turtles who thrust their necks skyward as they soaked up the early morning sunlight with eyes half closed, as if to ignore the other lake residents and their foolish dashing to and fro.

At the end of the lake we would descend slightly through a cool-green part of the forest. where ferns grew abundantly and where you could always feel a definite drop in temperature. Here also were broad-leaved trees, and the leaves that had fallen colored the path brightly as we came in sight of the little settlement. As we strode into the yellow dirt road that ran through the village, the local dog population would begin its dutiful yapping, announcing to the villagers that "someone was coming." We always headed straight for the little general store, because we never felt that our morning was complete without receiving our "sunshine smile" from smilin' Billy.

As we "clomp, clomped" side by side along the old wooden boardwalk with the rustic, handpolished sapling banisters, we felt almost like intruders upon the morning stillness. Somewhere in the village a rooster would crow, announcing to the residents that "these folks are right, it's time to get up and get with it". As we turned right, into the store, we always had to take "one giant step" over old Buffy the town pooch, who had long ago established his importance and seniority by "flopping" right in the middle of the doorway where you had to step over him in order to enter or leave the premises. Ahh, that smell of coffee, and spices, and new lumber that permeated our nostrils. How unlike the supermarkets it all seemed. How vibrant and real were the rich odors of new leather harness and freshly cut sassafras. And how appropriate to this setting of "reality" and "face value truth" was the presence of "Smilin' Billy."

They say his parents died when he was only seven; something about a car wreck in which they had slid off the rain-flooded mountain road, plummeting to their deaths in one of the deep gorges that paralleled so many of these winding, treacherous, and vulnerable mountain roadways.

Mr. Kramer, who owned the general store, had taken Billy in without fanfare. There was no formal adoption, no red tape, just a simple "You can move in with me, Billy. I have a spare room at the back of the store and you can help out a little bit when I get busy."

It had been a good association. Billy loved the old man and had himself grown into a strong, willing helpmate to the gentle Mr. Kramer. Billy had become the son that Mr. Kramer never had, but more than that, he had become the focus of Mr. Kramer's love and fond respect. You could see it in his eyes. Billy couldn't speak. No one seemed to know why. He had been taken to numerous doctors in an effort to determine the cause for his muteness, but the results were always the same. "There's nothing wrong with the boy, he just doesn't want to learn how to talk." It had been hard at first for Mr. Kramer to accept these findings, but as time went on he had decided almost without thinking about it that "if that's the way Billy wants it — that's the way it'll be." It was an experience in "soul communication" to watch the two of them. Mr. Kramer would say "Billy, will you bring in that keg of nails when you get time?" And Billy would smile broadly as if he had been awarded a chance to perform before royalty.

There was something striking, even memorable about Billy's appearance. He wore the old-fashioned bib overalls and the matching blue denim hat which always seemed to be "just slightly off-center" from the alignment of his face. His clothes looked as though they had just come from the laundry, and his face always wore that freshly scrubbed, brightly angelic smile for which he was famous. His blond curly hair was forever escaping the confines of the blue denim cap, and bouncing jubilantly about the area above his right eyebrow. His days were spent in carrying groceries to the cars and horsedrawn wagons of the store patrons. He would not accept a tip from anyone. When it was offered, he would shake his blond head vigorously, smiling broadly, and causing the curls to bounce about his forehead like golden ringlets, designed by some great artist to frame the brightness of his smile.

The magic warmth that belonged to smilin' Billy was his, and his alone. Never in my life have I seen the "raw" sincerity or the total open regard for others that shone upon that young mountain lad's face.

It was a smile that said, "Please, can I help you?" and "I like you a lot" and "I hope you come back soon" and when entering the store "Gee, it's good to see you." Yet he spoke not a word.

I saw him cry only once. Buffy had become ill for a few days, apparently from an overabundance of the little candies that the children liked to feed him. Billy lay right in the doorway with him for two days, stroking the large, fluffy head lovingly. His eyes were moist and red, but he still managed to smile through it all to the many friends he had, who came to see how Buffy was doing. As I remember that time, I can recall clearly the childlike innocence that only he had been allowed to keep well into his twenties. I can still see the small tears at the corners of his eyes as he would smile broadly, imploring you with his trust to "make Buffy get well," not unlike a small child who beseeches his father to mend a favorite broken toy.

He had retained, somehow, the clear-eyed openness that disarms and melts away even the most advanced cases of "protective aloofness."

Everyone was his friend, even the children who came into the store. There was an air about him that made you want to protect him from the unpleasant realities of life, to reinforce his unique and beautiful perspective of the world around him. He became our friend, and we shall never forget him.

There was a small white church a few doors down from the general store, and it had an "old-fashioned" church bell which had become the local alerting system for everything from Sunday worship to town meetings. We had heard it many times during our morning walks and on special occasions; its clear but slightly "off-tone" pealing would penetrate the evening stillness to announce that "something's going on at the village." It had, within its distinctive tone, a strange, compelling mysticism which seemed to reflect the urgency of the bell ringer as though it were forged by magic hands. I can hear it yet in my mind, ka-ding, ka-ding, ka-ding it would say, drawing the mountain people to it, like a huge magnet.

One evening, as we sat watching the finger-like shadows creep over the scenic valley that cradles Lake Mary, the bell began to peal. We listened attentively as its prolonged ringing echoed throughout the vast maze of canyons and mountains and endless forest.

Jackie spoke our thoughts first. "I wonder what that's all about," she said. After considering obvious possibilities in my mind for a moment, I replied.

"Well, it's not a fire, we would have seen the smoke by now."

"Maybe they're having a prayer meeting tonight," she countered.

"Not a chance, that bell has been ringing for a solid ten minutes. I think I'll call the general store."

"Well, ask them if they have any green thread while you're on the phone."

"Yeah, sure kid, sure."

"Hi, Mr. Kramer. This is Rog Vanderlaan at the far end of the lake. What's all the bell ringing for?"

"Well, Mr. Vanderlaan, our mayor, Mr. Sinclair, was found dead in his home about four o'clock this evening. He was well-known in the valley, and we want everyone to know that services will be held at the cemetery behind the church at ten-thirty tomorrow morning."

"What happened Mr. Kramer, was there an accident?"

"Oh no, no, nothing like that. He had a heart problem and I guess it just 'hit him' while he was alone."

"Well thank you, Mr. Kramer, we'll certainly be at the service."

"You're welcome — good night."

I hung up the phone and thought about the brief conversation. Jackie was not willing to wait for my "writer's evaluation."

"Well???"

"Well what?"

"Well, what's going on, why all the bell ringing?"

"Oh, Mr. Sinclair, the mayor passed away today. They're

having the service at ten-thirty tomorrow morning. I told them we would be there."

She digested that information slowly and then remarked quite casually, "Did they have any green thread?"

"Why yes, my Darling," I answered, "I ordered a nine foot ball of it; they're going to roll it over in the morning."

"Oh you smart aleck," she said, "How'd you like to fix your own supper tonight?"

"No thanks, and I'm sorry about the thread, it completely slipped my mind."

"Yeah, sure kid, sure," she responded.

The next morning was the first time since we had come to the mountain that I wore a suit. It felt somehow out of place and uncomfortably pretentious amidst the natural majesty of our summer home. Jackie was also dressed in her "Sunday-go-to-meetin'" clothes, but she managed to look cool and comfortable, and I might add, quite lovely.

The walk to the village was slow and dignified. No throwing mud clods at each other today. No trying to "bump" one another into the soft mud that bordered the lake. The dogs which were usually yapping their heads off as we approached the village, chose to remain silent, and contented themselves instead with "staring" at us as if they understood the solemnity of the occasion.

Everyone assembled at the small cemetery directly behind the old white church. As the mourners stopped arriving, the local preacher began his service.

"Dear friends," he announced, "We are gathered here to pay our last respects to a dear, departed soul. Chester Sinclair was a man who gave a great deal of his time, energy, and financial support to the people of this village." (I watched the little girl in the white dress and black patent leather shoes directly across the casket from me, begin to pick her nose.) "The very land that this church is built upon was given to this village by Chester Sinclair. He was always in the forefront of progress and worked tirelessly to make this village a pleasant place to live for all of us." (The little girl had succeeded in her task, and was now looking for someplace to put it.) "The poplar trees that line the far end of the street were planted by Mr. Sinclair; the new electric water pump that provides pressure for the village was a gift from Chester Sinclair." (Oops, I was afraid of that, right on the little white dress!) "I can think of no individual who has contributed more to our way of life than Chester Sinclair. He will be missed by all of us."

I glanced around the assembly of mourners, trying to find a sad face. I could not find one. As the preacher droned on, I gathered from his lengthy account that Chester Sinclair had indeed given much in the way of material assistance to the village. But why was no one crying? Where were the broken hearts, the inconsolable sobbing? There was a lady standing near the casket trying to "pop" her chewing gum. She was staring dry-eyed at the casket, apparently unaffected by the whole scene. And a man in a blue suit, just to her right, kept glancing at his watch. Another man was swinging at a persistent horsefly, while yet a third man was kicking over a tumble bug with the toe of his shoe.

I didn't get it. Here was a man who had, from all accounts, given generously of his finances on more than one occasion, and yet — I couldn't find a tear being shed on his behalf.

After the service we walked slowly back to the cabin, contemplating, I suppose, the finality of death and the realization that our days are numbered. Finally, Jackie spoke what was on both our minds.

"That has to be the strangest funeral I ever attended."

"I'll drink to that."

"Where were the grief-stricken relatives and friends?" she asked.

"I don't know, honey, I just hope somebody has the courtesy to blow their nose real loud when I go, or make some kind of noise to indicate that it's not "business as usual."

She gripped my hand a little tighter, and we walked the rest of the way back to the cabin without comment.

The remainder of the summer passed all too swiftly. With the early fall season practically upon us, we began to make plans for our return to Santa Barbara. The ski lodges at Mammoth and other nearby winter sport havens were already gearing up for the tourists.

The nights were getting downright chilly, and there hung a haze of "woodsmoke" in the air each morning. After dark, the landscape was dotted with small campfires, and the laughter of young adventurers could be heard drifting through the black, "spooky" forest until the early morning hours.

We attended several "barn dances" given by the village people, and enjoyed ourselves immensely. We were enchanted by the "folksy" atmosphere of these gatherings. It was fun both to square dance to the country music and to sit back a few feet from the dance floor to watch the swirling, graceful dancers in their blue jeans, bright shirts, calico dresses, and "flared" skirts. The music was of course strictly country. The guitars, fiddles, and the great old-fashioned "bass fiddle" thumped out a heavy rhythm that would set your toe to tapping in spite of yourself. These occasions were always preceded by delicious barbeques, guaranteed to enslave you forever to outdoor country cookin'.

At one of these affairs, I saw smilin' Billy sitting next to the bandstand with Buffy. He was smiling broadly as always and before the evening was over, I'm sure everyone who attended the dance stopped by to pet Buffy and say, "How ya doin', Billy." They were great days, the kind that stand forever in the memory as highlights of the goodness of life.

The sadness came like someone throwing ice-cold water in our faces.

We had just finished our coffee, preparatory to the morning walk. Jackie remarked about the coolness of the days, now that summer was about to end. I can recall saying, "I could see my breath this morning, time to start thinking about Santa Barbara," and then we heard it — The Bell.

It sounded different this time. Its ringing was slow, measured, almost melancholy. I spoke first.

"Well, who's going to call this time, me or you?"

"I'll call," she said.

As she waited for a reply at the other end of the line, I could see her nervously "chewing" one side of her mouth as she often did when she was upset. I could only hear one side of the conversation, but I knew at once that it was not Mr. Kramer who was on the phone.

She listened intently, and then I heard her say very softly, "Oh no."

Presently she replaced the phone on its hook, and sat quietly staring at the floor. I could see her blinking to keep back the tears. When she looked up at me, her eyes were moist and she spoke with a weak, sad voice.

"It's Billy, honey. He died last night."

"Oh my God!"

We both sat silently, waiting for the numbness to go away. The following day we packed up our belongings, with the exception of our dress clothes which we needed for Billy's funeral services.

Everything was scheduled for two o'clock that afternoon.

As we walked the familiar path to the village, my wife was crying softly. I tried not to break down and give way to the anguish and pain that I was feeling. It wasn't easy. In spite of the lateness of the season, it was a warm and beautiful day. As we approached the village, we were stunned by the large number of people who were milling about the small settlement. We made our way to the cemetery, along with several hundred other people, and waited patiently as the mourners continued to stream in.

How different this was from the last time. When the preacher began to speak, his voice was shaky and unsteady. He appeared to be close to losing control once or twice during the services. There was weeping on every side. Both the young and the old alike were sobbing deeply. It was hard to grasp the enormity of this tragic loss. I heard very little of what the preacher said. I was alone with my thoughts about smilin' Billy.

"Oh you magnificent young man," I was thinking. "You have touched and brightened the lives of all these people." — "you have confounded the logic of the world and without saying a word, you have taught us all the power of love." — "You have shown us our own great need, and you have proven beyond the slightest doubt that the truly pricelsss gifts we can bestow upon one another are from the depths of our soul. Who were you, young mountain boy, and which of God's creations will you now grace with your wonderful smile?" — "I won't forget you, nor will I forget the lessons that you have taught me. Goodbye my friend, we will miss you."

Jackie and I walked slowly back to the cabin. We loaded our belongings into the car, barely speaking. As we started down the mountain road, I thought about some of my own ambitions and plans. They seemed hollow and lifeless compared to the success story I had just witnessed. How few of us can hope to aspire to the purity of spirit that I chanced to encounter in the High Sierras.

I know one thing — Smilin' Billy was a great success.

Attitude Is The Foundation

Hopefully, we have established the fact that "success" and great wealth are not necessarily one and the same. I do feel compelled, however, to point out another great truth, and that is as follows: *There is absolutely nothing wrong with wanting to be financially well off, or even rich.*

The danger lies in mistaking "riches" for success. So long as we realize that money can be a very comfortable asset, but is by no means a guarantee of success, we can proceed with a proper perspective. The money then becomes a "tool" to be utilized in the pursuit of our goals, and not an end in itself. With this thought in mind, we can more clearly see the need for identifying, and then plotting a course toward, our own specific goals.

If you live on a small farm, for example, and you love the life and the good "down-to-earth" people, many of whom you may have known since childhood, perhaps the lure of "fancy places" or "hifalutin" people holds absolutely no attraction for you whatsoever. Maybe you wouldn't trade places, or the friendships you have made for anything on earth. Your goal may be to "get the kids through college" and to live out your life as a good friend and neighbor to the people you love. If that be the case, then you have already found what many others spend a lifetime searching for. Money is not a necessary "tool" for the goals of your life. In fact, it might even serve to alienate you from the life and the people that you love.

On the other hand, if your goals include traveling abroad with the love of your life, lengthy vacations in exotic places, the ability to "pick up and go" whenever you feel like it, or any other expensive passion, you will need the "tool" of money.

As you set your sights on the things you want to accomplish, your "attitude" concerning your ability to achieve them will either propel you forward at an astonishing rate, or destroy your chances for success before you ever get off the ground.

I want to spend a little time on that one, because I have known so many in life who had the grandest plans imaginable, but who later let it all slip away—because of their attitudes.

Let's assume that the goals of your life will require "the money tool." And let's further assume that you are presently at "ground zero" in that department. In other words—you don't have any, your parents don't have any, and there is no one you can turn to for a financial "boost."

Your attitude is immediately called upon to make an evaluation of the situation. If your response is negative, you will kill off your own chances for success before you ever get started.

The following would be negative responses:

- "Well, I just don't have the money to start that little business right now—maybe later." (Later never comes.)

- "Times aren't too good right now—what if I fail and everyone makes fun of me?" (There is never an ideal time to start a business.)

- "I'm sure the bank wouldn't loan me any money for this project, I was pretty slow repaying the last loan." (You're probably right. Banks are in business to help themselves.)

Obviously there will be very little accomplished with an attitude like that.

The first lesson you would need to learn is *"faith."* Faith in God to help you with your plans; faith in yourself to carry them out; and the courage to try, and if need be to try again, and again.

Your second step would be **the immediate replacement of all negative thoughts with positive thoughts.** It works like this:

- "Well, I just don't have the money to start that little business right now—maybe later."

Wait a minute—that's hogwash, what am I saying? Thousands of other people have started businesses who were just as broke as I am. It's a damn good idea and I know I can make it work. The time is now."

- "Times aren't too good right now—what if I fail and everyone makes fun of me?"

"Hold it!! There will always be good times and bad times, and what do I care if others scoff. At least I will have tried, which is more than most people do. Besides, when I'm successful the laughing will stop."

- "I'm sure the bank wouldn't loan me any money for this project, I was pretty slow repaying the last loan.

"On the other hand, who needs them. Tomorrow I will make a list of everyone I know who has a few bucks and makes investments, then I'll call them for an appointment. I'll lay out the whole project for them, pay them darn good interest, and get the money I need. If I call on twenty people, I should get enough to get started. If not, I'll call on twenty more."

Get the idea, reader? You don't allow *negative* thoughts to take root, you replace them at once with *positive* thoughts and then you **get on** with your project.

You may be saying to yourself, "Well, you've got to be realistic" or something to that effect. My friend, **you** are what's real, **and** your dreams, but they require that you breathe life into them, and you can't do that by looking for legitimate reasons for failure, or trying to justify your own lack of action. As George Bernard Shaw once wrote,

"People are always blaming their circumstances for what they are. I don't believe in circumstances. The people who get on in this world are the people who get up and look for the circumstances they want, and if they can't find them, make them."

Mrs. Warrens Profession
(Act II)

One final comment on *"replacing negatives."* This is a habit you will want to cultivate for use on a **daily basis,** not only while you are trying to establish a business or begin the pursuit of your goals. Remember that *"As a man (or woman) thinketh, so he, or she, is,"* or as another writer has put it, *"What the mind can conceive, and believe, it can achieve."* In short, there is no room in the makeup of positive, goal-striving individuals for negative, destructive thoughts.

Overcoming Faulty Programming

There is yet a third step you may have to take in order to "clear the decks" for your new approach to success. At an earlier point in this book, we made mention of the *"faulty implants"* that many of us carry around in our subconscious as the result of accepting opinions, comments, or indoctrination from our primary instructors when we were young and impressionable.

This is one of the hardest tasks we will have to face. It means we will have to re-examine some of the things we have always been told, always believed, and always accepted as fact. It is painful, in that it involves the "clearing away" of misconceptions that have been a part of our own thoughts for most of our lives. We can liken this process to the act of removing a tree stump from the midst of a well-manicured lawn. It will involve the pulling-out of old roots which have spread in all directions from the base of the once highly regarded tree. That means the lawn will be disfigured, rearranged, and generally traumatized while the "improvements" are being made.

Moreover, we shall have to face the very real possibility that dearly beloved people from our past—*may have been wrong about many things.* As in all searches for the truth, we must begin the process by a cold, analytical examination of the available facts, rejecting all emotional prejudice. The starting point will be your own fears and your own feelings about yourself, and what you believe your limits to be.

In the first chapter of this book I warned you that it would not be easy to change the *"faulty implants"* that you may be carrying around inside of you. It will involve a reprogramming of shall we say "up-to-date" material? Be confident, however, that you can accomplish the task, and that you will be a far better prepared man or woman to pursue your own meaning of success.

I suggest we revert again to a true story as our best means of seeing all sides of the problem.

Terry

Young Terry Sanders was the type of employee that most "bosses" would give their "eye teeth" to have working for them. He was conscientious, bright, friendly, and well-liked by everyone. You never had to tell him more than once to do something, and his reputation for honesty and dependability had not gone unnoticed by the company he worked for. Three years ago, to the delight of everyone who knew him, he married Lisa Crawford, one of the young secretaries in accounting. Lisa was a vibrant, outgoing girl who had deep, disarming dimples and a personality that made you feel as though you had known her all your life. It was a match "made in heaven" as the saying goes, and when she left the office to have their first child, the entire office staff marched her proudly down to the car amid proclamations about the proper care and feeding of "our" baby.

Terry and Lisa were blessed with a fine healthy son, whom they called Stephan. A year later they had a little girl, and they named her Cheri. They were to all appearances the ideal young family, and they seemed to have the necessary ingredients for a happy, successful life together. As time went on,however, Terry had begun to feel the financial "pinch" created by the loss of Lisa's income as she settled down to the job of raising the two children. Like all young couples, they began to quarrel occasionally about a variety of subjects which, if examined closely, would prove to be the symptoms of the "real"problem—too much "month" at the end of the money.

But there was another problem that neither one of them

realized was there. Terry had been approached on two occasions by the management team at work. They felt that he would make an ideal "sales coordinator," and they made no bones about telling him that the job was his, along with a sizeable salary increase and sales bonuses—if he wanted it.

Oddly enough, Terry was frightened by the whole prospect. He had told Lisa about the offer, and she couldn't understand why he didn't "jump" at the chance to move up in the company. He had found himself "snapping" at Lisa every time the subject came up. At work, he would purposefully avoid running into anyone connected with the management team, and he spent large amounts of time running errands for anyone who needed supplies, or other "out-of-office" duties tended to. On some other occasions, he had taken to "wandering" around the local park, or to just sitting quietly in some restaurant sipping coffee. These actions were so out of character for Terry that even "he" was mystified by them. He found himself "daydreaming" about the activities of the former sales coordinator who had since moved on to a new position with the company, in a distant city. In his mind's eye he saw mental images of the man, addressing a room full of sales people, or "chewing out" some of the "least productive" salesmen. The images frightened him—and he didn't know why. The thought of standing in front of a large group of people and giving a speech caused his nerves to tremble, and his palms to sweat. The whole reaction angered him with his own lack of "guts." He needed the job desperately for the benefit of his growing family, and yet the prospect of being "on stage" to all of those people was so devastating to him that he almost wished they had never asked him to take the position in the first place.

Sharp gal that she was, Lisa knew something was holding him back. She chose her time carefully, waiting for a moment when he was relaxed and comfortable, and then she approached the subject tactfully.

> "Honey, what have you decided about the sales coordinator job? I haven't heard you mention it lately."
> Terry started to squirm noticeably.

"I really haven't thought about it much. I've been so busy running errands I haven't had time to think."

She looked directly into his eyes, pausing slightly before she spoke. Her voice was soft and confidential.

"Hey, remember me? I'm the gal you love, the one you always 'level' with. Now, what's the real problem? Don't you think you'd like the job?"

"Oh, it isn't that," he answered, "I'm just not sure I could handle it."

She thought about his answer for a moment.

"Are you scared?" she asked.

Her directness seemed to strike a responsive cord. He answered her slowly.

"Yeah—Yeah, I guess I am."

Lisa allowed the gravity of the moment to penetrate, and then she smiled directly at Terry and spoke up brightly.

"I have good news for you, my husband. I'm a little scared too, but I think I know what we can do about it."

"Oh, is that right?" Terry shot back somewhat sarcastically.

"Do you remember when my Dad was so concerned about one of his new sales reps?" she asked.

"Yeah, whatever happened to the guy?"

"Well," she cooed, "he's doing wonderfully now, Dad's so proud of him."

"O.K., Lisa, what's the punch line?" Terry demanded.

"My father has this 'performance consultant' that he sends his employees to on occasion. Apparently the guy is really great. I think you should go see him," she replied.

"Lisa, I'm not going to go see a 'shrink'."

"He's not a 'shrink', honey, he's a specialist in helping business-oriented people to overcome their hangups."

"I haven't got any hangups" he barked. "I just don't know if I can handle the job or not."

"Oh, come on," she said demandingly. "You've been running away from opportunity for two weeks now. It's time to 'face up' to the problem and to find out how you can cope with it. Denying that it's there won't solve a thing."

Terry was silent. When at last he spoke, his voice was low, but firm with resolve.

"All right Lisa, if you think there's a chance this guy can help me—I'll go."

The first appointment with Mr. Kane went very smoothly. He was not at all what Terry had expected. He was loose and friendly and had reassured Terry at their very first meeting that his problem was not unusual, and that they would easily overcome it together. After a number of conversations with Terry, Mr. Kane made a surprising announcement.

"Terry," he said, "I want you to allow me to hypnotize you."

"Why?" Terry inquired.

Mr. Kane was all business.

"Terry, there are some things we lock away in our minds for many years, even forgetting that they're there. Hypnotism is a way of *unlocking* those secret storage areas so we can see what has been 'filed there'. It's perfectly safe, and I believe it's important that we find out just what kind of information you're carrying around in that old 'computer' of yours. What do you say we give it a try next week?"

Terry agreed to let Mr. Kane try, and for the next several sessions he remembered very little about the visits except for the strong, understanding voice of Mr. Kane urging him to relax and go to sleep. He did find it strange to awaken from the experience on several occasions with his eyes and face quite damp. As though he had been crying.

One bright morning Terry popped into Mr. Kane's office all prepared to be hypnotized again.

"Well, doc," he said, "time for beddy-bye again?"

"Nope," the good doctor replied, "but you and I have a lot of talking to do Terrence my boy—and some of it may be a little rough."

The conversation began easily, lightly, and with a soft delving into the early years of Terry's life. Mr. Kane appeared to be heading nowhere in particular until the subject of Terry's father came up.

"You loved your father very much, didn't you Terry?"

"Oh sure, we did a lot of things together. He was a great sports enthusiast and probably one of the 'smartest' people I've ever known."

"Would you say that you 'respected' your father?"

"Of course! He taught me practically everything I know."

Do you feel that he was 'right' about most of the things he taught you?"

"Oh yes! He was honest and he thought things out pretty carefully before he made any decisions."

"You were only sixteen when he was killed, weren't you?"

"Yes."

"Terry, do you remember the time you and your father quarreled about 'your going to college'?"

Terry smiled widely.

"I sure do—that was a dandy. How do you know about that?"

"You told me."

"I did? When? Oh, I get it, while I was hypnotized, right?"

"That's right, Terry. You also mentioned that your father had a pretty mean temper."

"Well, he used to fly off the handle once in a while."

"And he used to say things that hurt your feelings, didn't he?"

"Yeah, but I don't think he really meant them."

"I'm glad you realize that, Terry. He **didn't** mean them, but there's one problem"

"What's that?"

"Your subconscious mind thinks that he **did** mean those things and that everything he said about you while he was mad is true."

Terry looked surprised. He thought for a minute and then answered crisply.

"I don't understand what you mean."

"Terry, your subconscious mind had trained itself over a period of time to *accept as true* anything your father told you. It never learned to make exceptions if your father was angry, or sad, or tired, or disgusted. It just automatically filed the information under 'true facts' without regard for the frame of mind that your father was in at the time."

"Yeah, but I know he didn't mean those things."

"Yes, but your subconscious mind **does not**—and that's what we've got to correct. The death of your father complicated the matter because your subconscious mind had grieved just as surely as you did, and then vowed to honor all that he had taught you— even though some of the information was not true."

"And you think that has something to do with my not wanting to accept the new position at work?"

"I'm sure of it, Terry. Think about that last big quarrel with your father. He called you stupid and said you would never be able to handle anything better than a janitor's job if you didn't continue on with your education, didn't he?"

Terry's eyes began to glaze as the memory of that last horrible argument came rushing back to him.

"'Yes, he said a lot of things like that."

"Well, don't you see, Terry? That's the problem. Your mind has 'believed' all of those things—that's why you're fighting yourself to keep from 'stepping up' in the world. It would be like a violation of what your subconscious mind has believed about your abilities all these years."

Terry began to weep, covering his face with his hands. Mr. Kane let him sob until he was sure that it was all out of his system.

"Are you all right, Terry?" he gently inquired.

"Yeah, except that I feel like a damned idiot. I didn't mean to blubber all over the place."

"Terry, let's face it. It feels good to 'let it all out' once in a while, doesn't it?"

"I guess," Terry laughed.

Mr. Kane was patient and understanding as he waited for Terry to compose himself. When he spoke again it was with an edge of determination in his voice.

"O.K., Terry, what we've got to do now is *reprogram* some current information into that marvelous computer of yours during the next few weeks, but I want you to think about something on your way home tonight. Your father wanted you to have the best possible chance at life that you could have. That's why he became so upset when he thought you were going to 'give up' on your education. He certainly wouldn't want you to 'limit' yourself because of a mistaken belief that you were honoring his predictions—you know that now, don't you?"

"Yes, I do."

"Then let's start turning it all around. We will honor your father's memory by helping you to achieve all of the things that he would have wanted for you, so long as they are things that **you** want as well."

The two men shook hands, and Terry strode into the coolness of the evening feeling relieved. As a matter of fact, he felt good— real good.

Subsequent meetings with Mr. Kane were geared largely

toward examining some of Terry's beliefs about himself. The probing intensity of Mr. Kane's directness and investigative questioning brought to light a number of long-forgotten incidents which the perceptive doctor would skillfully disassemble and then *rebuild* for Terry, until he was sure that any future remembrance of the subject would be viewed in a proper, positive frame of mind.

It was during one of these "fishing expeditions" that Mr. Kane discovered the source of Terry's great fear of speaking before a group of people.

As a boy, Terry had gone through a period of time in his life when he seemed to have lost control of his bladder function. When he found himself under stress, or fearful of some impending occurrence, he would wet his pants. The teacher entrusted with the furtherance of his education at that time was not overly sympathetic to the problem. Her reaction to one of these incidents was to "shame" him in front of his classmates, presumably to "frighten" him into not wetting his pants. It must have been a terrible experience for the boy, when on one such occasion she forced him to stand up in front of the class and read a lengthy report on "Our Park System in the U.S.A." (Terry had recalled the subject of the report during one of Mr. Kane's inquisitions.) We can only imagine at this point, the traumatic embarrassment he must have suffered as he stood there with his trousers wet, tears streaming down his face and classmates laughing heartlessly as he struggled to read the report.

Mr. Kane re-assembled the whole incident, made Terry suffer through it all one more time, and then slowly and methodically forced his young friend to re-evaluate the "true" picture of that event. Terry was made to realize that the teacher was acting out of ignorance, the children were reacting in a manner predictable for youngsters of that age, and "he", that is Terry, was in no way responsible for his involuntary physical functions at that unhappy time in his life.

Once the "source" of Terry's fear was removed, it became only a matter of time and practice before he developed into a very effective public speaker.

It's nice to be able to report to you that Terry and Lisa are both doing rather well. The restoration of Terry's confidence in himself, along with the guiding hand of Mr. Kane from time to time, have contributed substantially to his success. When a negative thought enters Terry's mind, he is quick to replace it with something *positive* these days. He has learned that he is just as "eligible" for the good things of this life as anyone else is, and now that Mr. Kane has shown him the way, he faces his fears "head-on" and begins at once to search for the *"reasons"* for them. His success from this time forward is merely a matter of time and easily predictable. Terry now realizes what many people spend their entire lives trying to discover. The secret of success lies *within*. The barriers to success are *within*. Your attitude, both conscious and subconscious concerning yourself, will determine the extent to which you will succeed in the pursuit of your own personal meaning of success. How wise were the ancient inscriptions on the temple at Delphi. They summarized in a very brief, yet poignant statement the "whole" of the secret to successful living. They translated to read very simply:

"Know Thyself."

Deprogramming Our Attitudes

Not all of us have the time, the inclination or the money to seek professional assistance when our intellect tells us that something we don't fully understand is holding us back. We are usually vaguely aware of the fact that it is some form of *"fear,"* but our tendency is to jump to the conclusion that—"I can't do so and so because I'm afraid"—or we will conjure up protective "reasons" for not making the attempt. Rarely do we go the one step farther to investigate the "cause" of that fear. In the beginning pages of this book I said that we would use *"truth* as our guidepost" as we examined the various aspects of our attitudes. I cannot overstress the importance of being totally and completely honest with yourself as a precondition to searching out the destructive *"implants"* that could very well be stifling your efforts to succeed at some task, or objective.

Before we continue, I want to remind you that many a lightly spoken word or phrase, when uttered by someone whom you had come to rely upon for truth and accuracy, may in fact now be a part of your attitude. With that thought in mind, let's examine some of the more common phrases that we have all been exposed to and see if they still "ring true" after all these years.

Faulty Implants

Don't try to be something you're not.
> Bad advice. Who knows what you can be if you will but try.

You can't make a purse out of a sow's ear.
> Wrong! It's been done.

You'll never amount to anything.
> No one can predict what you will "amount" to—unless you believe that statement to be true.

It was good enough for your father, and it's good enough for you.
> "Good enough" may not be "good enough" for you. You are not your father.

Who do you think you are?
> Implies that you're not really anyone very important.

Why can't you be like (whoever)?
> There's no one in this world quite like you. Follow your own dreams.

The rich get richer and the poor get poorer.
> If you believe that to be true, it will become a "self-fulfilling prophecy." The truth, however, is a totally different story. Never in the history of the world have so many people become rich, starting from "zero" as in the last ten years. These are the "good old days."

Stick to what you know.

"What you know" may never permit you to earn any more than a mediocre living. Step out and follow **your** dreams—now.

"It's a funny thing about life: If you refuse to accept anything but the best, you very often get it."
W. Somerset Maugham

Don't take foolish chances.

There is nothing "foolish" about striving to be the best that you can be. "As a man thinketh—so he is."

You just wait—some day you'll be sorry.

We have all made mistakes—but we cannot go through life grieving about them. What's done, is done. We're different people now, and we will act in accordance with our new knowledge.

I'm certain that you can easily remember many of these little "pearls of wisdom" from your own past. Some were given to us with the very best of intentions as a means toward "protecting" us from failure—some were not. All need to be examined for their *"truth content."* Surely, we can now realize that an attitude formulated with a constant barrage of *"negative implants"* such as the preceding, is one that has little likelihood of propelling the possessor toward brilliant achievement.

Our course of action is clear then. We must haul out and examine our fundamental beliefs about our abilities, capabilities and aspirations in the cool, clear atmosphere of this new-found knowledge. We need to ask ourselves **why** we don't believe that we can do this or that. Furthermore, we must be willing to "throw on the scrap heap forever" those old and useless bits of indoctrination that we discover to be untrue—**no matter who taught them to us.**

The formula for this kind of "mental housecleaning" is simple.

If it's negative — get rid of it.

It takes effort and practice, but it can be done. You will find yourself in a state of "personal confrontation" throughout the course of your "changeover" period, but in the end you will learn to replace those thoughts that you recognize as being negative with new, positive, productive thoughts, and the change in your attitude will please you, as well as the people with whom you come into contact.

You will need to carry the process one step farther, and this final step will require that you develop an uncommon amount of "understanding," in that you will be scrutinizing very closely the *"truth content"* of any new information or advice given to you by your friends and associates.

Once you have formed the habit of thinking in "positive" terms and begun to embrace a "can do" attitude, you will be shocked at just how many people there are who can't seem to take a positive, optimistic stance on **anything.**

This is where the understanding comes in. You will have to remind yourself that most of your friends and associates were subject to the very same kind of *"negative implants"* that you were during their formative years. Moreover, you will find yourself annoyed, at the limited imagination and total lack of confidence exhibited by people whom you may well have known for the better part of your life. You will in fact, be seeing things and people from a completely different viewpoint. They will not have changed, but you will be a different person.

A friend may say, "Real estate? Oh God, you're not going to get mixed up in **that**, are you.? I have this couple I bowl with and they lost their shirt in real estate." And it will anger you slightly that your friend considers this a valid reason for avoiding real estate. You will also be secretly miffed because he or she has thrown a negative dart at your optimistic balloon.

As a matter of course, you will find yourself seeking out and associating with positive, goal-striving individuals. But don't forget the old friends. They, after all, are victims of the same kind of mental conditioning that you and I went through. Perhaps in our lifetime we shall see this practice changed. I am hopeful that as we realize the impact our early indoctrination has had on the remainder of our lives, we will begin to teach the young, through classes geared to the formulation of their attitudes, how "all important indeed" are the concepts of self-worth, deservedness, and uninhibited faith.

> *"To accomplish great things we must not only act, but also dream; not only plan, but also believe."*
>
> *Anatole France*

Lest the content of the message in this chapter be misinterpreted, I feel compelled to add the following notation:

Mothers and fathers, or other close loved ones are yet beyond question, the greatest source of training and caring that we shall ever encounter. Still, with the maturity of years comes the realization that they are after all part of the human family and therefore subject to mistakes, ommissions, and errors in judgement. An awareness of this reality in no way detracts from their irreplaceable value, any more than an acquired taste for German chocolate cake could negate the benefits of homemade apple pie.

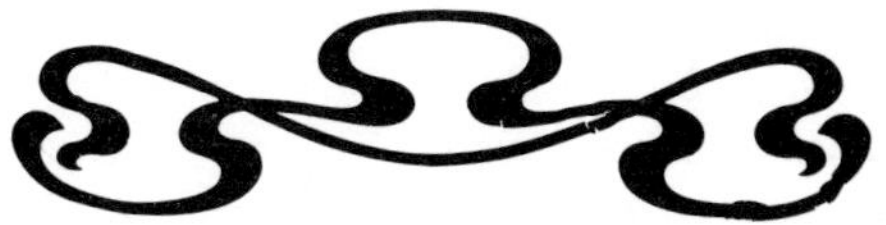

CHAPTER SEVEN

TURNING IT ALL AROUND

You will have arrived at a state in your life very similar in many respects to being reborn, once you have mastered the technique of investigating for *true worth* the substance of what you have learned in the past, as well as the *"new input"* that will come to you from many sources.

The vital difference will be that you will not allow those things suspiciously sounding like opinions, sour grapes, thoughtless comment and the like to become *"implants."* In other words, you will have learned to "throw out the garbage" and keep the groceries.

Relevant truths will now hold your attention, and mysteriously you will find that you have developed an uncanny ability to look for and discover the "real" reasons behind all manner of advice and comment that comes your way. It's called "insight," and it cannot function in your life until you have learned to look beyond surface comment to "hidden truth."

The process can be compared to cleaning out your garage. You've now gotten rid of all the junk and you're determined that no more will accumulate there. But what will you do with the empty space?

That's what this chapter is about. The reprogramming of your attitude.

I think a short review of some of our earlier subjects might be appropriate at this time—but remember—you are now going to examine everything that comes your way for its "truth content."

Faith In God

What does that really mean? Does it mean that God stands ready to jump in and do it all for you should you decide to try something new (like a new business)? Absolutely not!

God put us here to function, not to press the "God button" and foolishly hope that He will relieve us of all responsibility while we sit idly on the sidelines. I hate to break this to some of you, but, you're expected to get off your fannies and give it your very best shot—**then** God will help you. In other words, Faith, without works, is dead.

Faith In Yourself

I sincerely hope that everything we've discussed up to this point in the book has helped you to realize that you are capable of far more than you may have been led to believe. If you've never had much confidence in your own abilities, maybe it's time you started giving yourself a break.

Take that dream you've had for so long and **go** for it. You may be absolutely shocked at what you're able to do—if you will only try. Don't tell me you're a loser. I have seen too many lives turned around because people suddenly began to realize that they were entitled to the best—**just as you are.**

The Courage To Try

Please don't look for iron-clad guarantees before you begin whatever it is that you want to accomplish. There is a strange law in effect regarding success. You have to pay the price of *"never knowing."* I believe God designed it that way to teach us faith, in Him, and in ourselves. If we knew beforehand what the results would be, there would be no need for faith, courage, or effort. That's why I stated in an earlier chapter that an attitude which has not yet learned faith, is incomplete. But you can learn it—while you're trying.

With the preceding ingredients as our basic foundation, and with the knowledge that our attitudes can make or break us, let's set a format for the reprogramming of that "empty space" we were talking about.

POSITIVE NEW GOALS

Replace All Negatives

We've learned to replace negative thoughts with positive thoughts. Let's make it a prime ingredient of our new attitude toward ourselves, our abilities, and the things we are going to achieve. We can't move forward if we're forever stumbling over self-doubt, lack of confidence, or the mistaken belief that we are somehow not entitled to succeed.

Physical Condition

If you're not feeling well, do something about it. Not "some day," but as soon as possible. Find the problem and solve it, you no longer have room in your life for "poor health." You have much to accomplish. As Vince Lombardi has said, *"Fatigue makes cowards of us all."* Don't allow your plans to be threatened by this evil. Your spirit will rally to your cause when you set out to defeat this enemy of your dreams.

Forgive Yourself

Sure you've made mistakes and some of them were "whoppers," so what? That makes you part of the human race. It's time to forgive yourself and to realize that you're no longer the same person you were then. It is an absolute "must" that you "like" the person you have become in order to pursue your new goals. You can't possibly do that so long as you insist upon punishing yourself for past mistakes. The past is the past—forget it.

Forgive Others

Once you have forgiven yourself for past mistakes, it will

become much easier to forgive others. We often lash out at other people and their unsavory actions because of the suppressed desires of our own hearts. Our anger is really for ourselves. If we can then forgive the things we don't like about ourselves, we can far more easily learn to practice tolerance toward others. Let's face it, none of us are perfect. We have already seen how destructive anger can be. The only way to eliminate anger—is to forgive.

Work On Your Personality

After you've emptied your spirit of anger, you can begin to restructure your personality. If you are by nature a happy-go-lucky type of person, so much the better. (God knows we need more like you.) If not, here are a few thoughts for you. Not all of us are endowed with bubbling charm or sparkling personalities. It is probably just as well, however, that some of us tend to be a bit more on the serious side. Remember though that it isn't necessary to have an "ear-catching, side-splitting" sense of humor in order to have a great attitude. You will find on the other hand that "the more you do to improve your attitude" (as outlined in these pages) the more you will find to be good humored about.

Magnetic Conditioning

Don't forget our discussion on this subject. You will most definitely draw unto yourself reflections of the things you project. If you wish to be treated as a competent, confident person on the road to success, you will have to "project" that image. Guard against careless, thoughtless remarks or actions. You will be either a victim or the happy recipient of, *"reflective reactions."* Take care that your "projections" are tempered with love. It's a great reflection to receive from others. Remember, the other fellow's point of view is all important to him or her. Learn to listen—he or she will then be encouraged to help you.

The R. A. Factor

Be on the alert for those persons with a high R.A. factor. Don't allow your dreams to be destroyed by the reckless abandon of one of your associates or friends. Look to your own R.A. factor. You know what you can afford to venture, and what you must not put at risk. Distinguish between the two.

Prepare Your Mind For Success

You are now a new person and no longer a prisoner of your former limitations. For that reason you need to prepare yourself for success. The first step you will want to take (because it helps to make the other steps work more smoothly) is this: **Start acting like the person you want to become.** That's right. Begin to conduct yourself as though you had already achieved your goals. I can't overstress the importance of this step. It sets up a positive, confident approach to every move you make. It is as though you had embraced success as a definite part of your future and were now only waiting for the results to be tabulated. It indicates faith, it illustrates your unshakable belief in yourself, and it starts you out as a new person, no longer hampered by old conceptions. You will begin to act, dress, talk, walk, think, and function in a manner that will draw the positive aspects of your future right into your hands. I have a very wealthy friend who used to borrow money from me to buy groceries. In the old days (before he became wealthy) he used to smile at me good-naturedly and say, "I'm really very rich, I just haven't got the money yet." He went on to make millions. His secret was simple. He always believed that his station in life was that of a very successful and wealthy man—and he acted like it—even when he was broke. In the end, it all came to him—because he expected it.

Set Specific Goals

I know you've heard or read it before, but this time I'm hoping it will take root. There is no power whatsoever in a broad, general statement like the following:

"I know what my goal is—I want to be rich."

That's like a rookie baseball player saying, "I want to win ball games." Or a "would-be" auto racer saying, "I want to win races." That type of statement is a "wish," not a goal. A goal is something you set out to achieve, taking the necessary steps along the way to insure that you will ultimately be in the best possible position you can attain, favorable to the realization of that goal or goals. The rest of the process is dependent upon "the things of the spirit" such as your faith, determination, strength of character, commitment, and belief.

Before we pursue the subject of goals any further, let me remind you that this book is not being written to "help you get rich" period. It is being written to help you in the understanding of your own attitudes and by that process to enhance your ability to bring about the fruition of your own dreams. If one of those dreams is to be rich—fine, but make sure that it's what **you** want before you set your heart upon it.

There is a system whereby you can clarify the things you want to accomplish, and at the same time, examine them thoughtfully before you commit your energies to them. It works like this:

1. Write down all of the things you would like to accomplish.
2. Take them one by one and ask yourself these questions—Do I **really** want that? And what are the "bad" things that could happen if I got it? (Write them all down.) Call them negatives.
3. On a separate piece of paper entitled "positives," list all of the benefits you would enjoy upon reaching your goals. (Take them one by one.)
4. Compare the "positive" page against the "negative" page and you will have some idea as to the worth of your pursuits.

You may be surprised to discover that "it just isn't worth it," or that you really don't want some of the things you always thought you did.

You may also discover that by "scratching" the useless pursuits, the road becomes much clearer in the direction of the truly worthwhile goals.

Once you have arrived at a list of goals that you're excited about, put them all down on a 3x5 card that you can carry around with you. These are your **"ultimate goals,"** and your list may look something like the following:

1. Within five years from today, I will own two million dollars worth of real estate.
2. From this day forward I will begin to improve my relationship with my family and friends. I will no longer bear grudges or expect perfection from others.
3. I will begin at once to start acting like the person I want to become. I know that success is coming, and I must prepare myself for it.
4. I will begin to enjoy myself and to see that my family has a good life, before the children are grown and gone from me forever. I will not let my business goals interfere with my plans for the people I love.
5. I will remember to "give" every good thing that I can to others as I know that I will in some way be rewarded, and reap the benefits of "liking" myself for the kind of person I have become.

The list of course is very personal in nature and can only be written by you. It can be as long or as short as you wish, but must contain the ultimate things you are going to achieve.

Now you will take a second 3x5 card and list upon it your **short-term goals.** This list is nothing more than a written road map to help you accomplish your long-term goals and will change often as you reach certain plateaus. Notice if you will how the short-term goals compliment the larger ultimate goals.

1. I will get my hands on and read everything I can find regarding the purchase of real estate.
2. I will enroll in a real estate class at the first opportunity.
3. I will attend any open meetings that relate to real estate.

4. I will take the family to the mountains during my vacation. I will inform them in advance, so they can start looking forward to it.
5. I will take the whole family out for pizza this week.

I'm sure you get the idea by now. With this kind of planning, every step you take is in the direction of your goals. How much more sensible than a vague, wistful approach like "I want to be rich."

Having established what it is that you want to accomplish, there's one more thing you will need to do. Take your goal cards out and read them every day. I said **every** day. Without getting overly technical about it, you will be constantly reminding yourself of your purpose and you will be bringing your short-term goal list up-to-date as you achieve the steps one by one. I like to read my goal list just before retiring. It gives my subconscious mind something to work on while I sleep. Remember, specific goals, not vague wishes.

Set A Deadline

Now you have a definite pattern to establish, a positive approach to follow as you reprogram your attitude with new and exciting *"implants."* There remains one thing to be done in order to make it all come together. You need to set a "deadline" for beginning the whole process. Not "Sounds good, maybe I'll try that," or "One of these days I'm gonna try those ideas," but a definite starting date to begin. I would suggest one week to the day after you finish reading this book. That will give you time to establish your goals, reread some of the areas you want to refresh your memory on, and generally consider the value of the things we have talked about. So, the day you put this book down—go and circle the calendar in bold red ink for a day one week in advance. That's the day you start **turning it all around.**

The Good News

I have tremendously good news to give you. When you have finally determined to change your life for the better and to step out with positive new goals, you are going to be absolutely astounded at the many "great new forces" you will suddenly find working in your favor. You will soon discover that you have tapped a reservoir of power you probably never even suspected was there before. The great thinkers of the ages have seen it, so have the more sensitive poets, artists, playwrights, and philosophers. They have mentioned it in countless works over the centuries. The message is clear: Man is by nature a goal-striving creature, and the "greatness" that dwells within the heart of man can only be released by bold, strong steps in the direction of his dreams.

> *Whatever you can do, or dream you can,*
> *begin it.*
> *Boldness has genius, power and magic in it.*
>
> *Goethe*

There is a freedom of spirit akin to the soaring of an eagle for those precious few who renounce decisively the bondage of fear and choose instead to stride courageously into the great arena of sought-after dreams. Theirs is a life of electrifying fullness, of spiritual fellowship with the fates. They live on the brink of their own faith and they laugh into the teeth of the storms of life. Such is the company you will be keeping when you circle that date on the calendar and resolve to live life to the fullest, in place of fearfully waiting for your portion of the handouts.

You will also become aware of surprising changes in your attitude, concerning a great variety of subjects and activities, such as sports, television, social functions, movies, plays, parties, and the like.

No longer will you be content to live out your dreams vicariously. The strong will to control and create the conditions of your own destiny will suffer the short-sightedness of others very lightly, and the "profits of doom" who abound in great numbers will not perpetrate fear in your heart but rather, insightful tolerance.

Others will be drawn to you perceptively. Strength has a way of "showing through," and those who are lacking in this regard will gravitate to your side without really knowing why. You will find them strangely accommodating and eager to help you in the pursuit of your goals. The reason is not easily defined, but, the world loves a winner. It allows them a chance to share in the victories without taking the risks. Secretly, they admire and respect you—and usually wish they had the courage to do as you are doing. When the world observes the actions of an uncommon man or woman who has "strength of purpose" as their driving force, it stands spellbound on the sidelines, fascinated by the magic sequence of events that seem to assemble themselves in collective support for that courageous spirit.

Once you have established a definite destination, you will find your energies focused steadfastly on the road that leads to it. You will be able to transfix the most stubborn of obstacles and to avoid superfluous, time-wasting detours. You will in fact, by reason of your clarity of vision, develop a remarkable propensity for doing the right thing, at the right time.

As a matter of automatic procedural conditioning, you will one day realize that *there can be no failure for the determined spirit*. To be sure, you will have your setbacks, disappointments, lack-luster results, etc., but you will see them for what they are. They will not deter you from your purpose. They will only serve to strengthen your resolve, and to deepen your commitment in the pursuit of your dreams.

The simple act of refusing to accept failure will set you apart from the great multitude of the world's peoples as distantly as is the sun from the moon. Having embraced the whole of the concept of self-worth and self-deservedness, your attitude will now begin to "work wonders" for you as those things designed by the great hand of God to "test" the metal of your spirit begin to appear as if out of nowhere. Recognize them for what they are. Know that they are the stepping stones required for the advancement of your character, and know also that they have a solution which it is within your power to discover.

A short study of the lives of those persons whom we have all come to respect and admire, the ones who have contributed the greatest amount of good to mankind, will reveal to us a remarkable similarity in the "pattern" of their lives. They all have had to overcome an assortment of difficulties on the road to their successes. Some were financial, some personal or physical, and many were repeat performances of the ongoing battle between men of vision and dreams and men of short-sighted arrogance or ignorance.

Nothing has really changed. The battle remains one of "spiritual conflict." On the one hand we have men and women who act and react out of fear. On the other we have the visionaries and dreamers who dare to plant their feet solidly in the good earth of faith and courage. God spare us from a day when the intellectual security of our society takes precedent over the cultivation of our dreamers to the extent that they are no longer encouraged to dream great dreams. Mankind will have snuffed the candle of his own spirit in that day, and the robotic inhabitants of this planet will have little in common with the creative magnificence of their ancestors.

There is another bit of good news I want to share with you. Freedom of the spirit is the mother of creative genius. In your new role as a person in search of his or her dream, you are going to be quite surprised at some of the ideas you come up with, along with the frequency of their occurrence. It's almost as if you had opened a door to higher intelligence. The actual reason has to do with the clearing away of earlier inhibitions. The ability was there all the while, but you were afraid to use it. Now—the sky's the limit. If it's in keeping with the achievement of your goals, you will jump right in and go to it, whereas in the past you would have spent useless energy trying to justify reasons why "it won't work." What a great time you're in for. There is absolutely nothing I can think of as satisfying as watching your own dreams come true, step by step, according to your plan. It's an exhilerating "high" that brings a smile to your face and a cheer to your heart. I'm rooting for you, and I know you can do it. Go get 'em.

Enhancing Your Chances

I have spent a goodly amount of time on the subject of "starting your own business" as I know that a great many of the dreams people dream in this wonderful land of opportunity, are rooted in the American tradition of starting with an idea and watching it grow, limited only by the extent of the dreamer's imagination. I do wish to recognize, however, that "not all visions of success are centered around a desire to be self-employed."

On the contrary, many people have found their respective niches in life as a functioning "part" of a larger "whole." Some love the politics, intrigue, and competitive spirit of corporate structure. Still others prefer the stability and familiar faces of the "small business" atmosphere.

Whatever your preference, you will have to decide at some point in your life whether or not you are successful, by your own definition of that term.

Obviously, if you are perfectly content with things as they are, there will be no need for change. If, on the other hand, the desires of your heart are not being met, I suggest you do something about it.

I will tell you the story of "Karen" in the hope that you may draw some parallels to your own life, possibly crystallizing your goals in the process.

Karen:

She had long, silken black hair, her most prominent feature. Her skin was fair, and her eyes a startling blue. She had a tendency to dress in bright reds or greens, and nature had blessed her with a warm smile, friendly disposition, and straight white teeth.

When I first met Karen, she worked for a well-known local attorney as a receptionist. She was twenty-two years of age at the time.

There was one unfavorable feature about Karen's makeup. She was considerably overweight. The condition had caused a strange reaction in her attitude, resulting in the formation of the most "apologetic" creature I had ever known.

I'll swear to you. That young lady was apologizing for

"something" with every other breath. It would take an adept study of her psyche I suppose to accurately identify the progression of events that had brought her to that state, but the over-simplified impression that I received from her was one of an attractive young girl who felt terribly guilty about the way she had allowed her "poundage" to get out of control. In my opinion the apologies were really for her overweight condition, although they took the form of "scattered buckshot" regrets for anything and everything in sight.

Fate had decried that we would meet often, as her boss was my business attorney. As time went on, I had developed the habit of eating lunch at the little Italian restaurant on the first floor of the office building in which he had his practice. From there it was a simple matter to mount the elevator to the fourth floor in plenty of time for our ritualistic 2:00 p.m. appointments.

Karen also ate her lunch there, because of the proximity to her work, and soon we had become friends, sharing not only the excellent Italian cuisine, but an open, respectful brother-sister relationship which I treasure to this day. I found myself "nipping away" at her "out-of-focus" opinion of herself, and I'm afraid I was a pretty picky lunch partner during the early days of our friendship. After we had grown to know each other, and after I had given her a number of thinly disguised lectures on self-esteem, our conversations went something like this:

Karen: Hi Rog, I'm sorry I'm late.

Rog: Karen, you're not late, don't apologize.

Karen: We're so busy upstairs you wouldn't believe it.

Rog: I can imagine.

Karen: I was working on *your* file most of the morning. Frankly, I didn't get it finished. Sorry, Rog.

Rog: I wouldn't have known it if you hadn't brought it up. Don't apologize.

Karen: I think I'll just settle for the pastrami sandwich, I'm not very hungry.

Rog: Well, lunch is on me, so "dig in."

Karen: Oh, I didn't expect you to buy lunch, Rog, did you think I was hinting?

Rog: No, Karen, I didn't think you were hinting, now eat hardy.

Karen: Well, I'm really not very hungry, sorry Rog.

Rog: Karen, don't apologize because you're not hungry.

Karen: Well, I'm sorry if you thought . . .

Rog: **KAREN!!**

Karen: OK, OK. I'm sorry — oops, I mean, well — OK.

By this time she was laughing, amused by the realization that she had been apologizing with every other sentence.

Slowly, over a period of time, she began to replace her apologies with interesting, thoughtful conversation. I discovered that she had an ongoing love affair with "little theatre" work and that her secret desire was to be an actress. She had not as yet learned to make it a goal.

I also learned that she had given up her "little theatre" work when she had begun to gain weight. She admitted openly to me that she was ashamed of her overweight condition and that she felt terribly self-conscious in front of an audience.

I realized that she was searching for ways to justify failure. We talked about it many times. I also knew that nothing would change until she felt that she was taking steps in the direction of her dreams. I attacked her reasons for not doing so relentlessly.

She had accumulated an impressive collection of damn good reasons for failure. Among them, as I recall, were the following:

—I hate to leave Mr. Schaefer, he's such a great boss.
—It would take the office a year to train my replacement.
—Everything's so convenient here.
—I'd miss this great little restaurant.
—It's only 20 minutes from home to work.
—You don't make any money in theatre unless you're exceptional.
  The list went on and on.

She had settled into a comfortable little rut where she could get by easily without much effort or work — and she was afraid to leave it. The price she had paid for her secure, effortless routine was a great one. She had traded her dreams, and now her ambition for those dreams was slowly slipping away.

I mounted a full-out attack, criticizing every reason she gave for not getting on with the pursuit of her own personal goals and forcing her to face the realities of the choice she was making.

"Karen, I know you're a great secretary, but I want you to face the truth. As valuable as you are to Mr. Schaefer, two months from the time you leave that office it will be business as usual. You are not irreplaceable—none of us are. You have fallen into a routine that is slowly stripping you of your own ambitions."

After a reflective pause, she had answered slowly.

"I know you're right—but I really don't know what to do about it." (I was ready for that one.)

"I think I do, Karen, if you'll listen to me." I looked her directly in the eye while she thought about it, saying nothing and awaiting her reply.

Cautiously she responded. "All right, I'll listen."

"Good!! Here's what we'll do." I reached inside my left breast pocket and produced a blank 3x5 card.

"I want you to take this card home with you tonight and write down the things you would like to be doing five years from today, if you could be doing anything you wished for. Don't be embarrassed, tell it like it is. I will meet you here next Thursday for lunch and we'll go on to step two. Agreed?"

"Well, OK, if you say so, but don't laugh at my notes."

"I won't laugh, Karen."

She had excused herself shyly, placed the card inside her purse, and left the table with a friendly "See you next Thursday."

Having been privy to some of her almost forgotten dreams, I knew what the next step would be. I prepared the details during the remainder of the week.

The following Thursday, I entered the restaurant at exactly 12 noon. My eyes scanned the room searching for the familiar long black hair which set her apart so distinctly from the rest of the crowd. When at last I located her, I was pleased to see that she was concentrating heavily on the 3x5 card I had given her at our last luncheon. She had chosen to sit near the decorative red and gold wall at the far side of the restaurant.

I made my way through the tables of busy, laughing patrons accompanied by the metallic staccato of cheap table silver rattling the atmosphere from all directions.

"Hi Karen, have you ordered?"

"Not yet," she smiled, "I don't have to return to the office until 2:00 — I thought we might want to talk awhile."

"May I see your list of goals?" I inquired.

She handed the list to me slowly, the way you would release your car keys to a casual friend.

I smiled reassuringly. "Don't worry, I won't bite your hand."

She laughed good-naturedly, confirming the reciprocal trust that was part of our friendship. "You promised not to laugh," she reminded me.

We were interrupted by the middle-aged waitress.

"Would you like a cocktail, Mr. Vanderlaan?"

"No thanks, but perhaps the young lady would like one."

"Oh no, thanks," Karen responded, "but the meatball sandwich looks good, and a cup of coffee."

"Make that two orders," I added.

Karen had written three goals on her list. I can tell you the rest of the story, but I have promised that her identity will remain a secret. The goals were:

One—To have my own business—preferably a women's weight loss center.

Two—To be a recognized actress.

Three—To be involved with "little theatre" productions.

I smiled as I read the goal list. Her expression remained blank.

"Karen, I think these are great. But now we must go to the second step." I handed her the card, along with my black marking pen. "We will now change these 'wishes' to goals. At the top of your list in bold black letters, I want you to write the words 'Personal Goal List.'"

She did so without comment.

"Now I want you to start a second card called 'Immediate Goals.' I have taken the liberty of starting one for you." I reached inside my coat pocket and produced the second card. I withheld it briefly as I explained its purpose. "This card will be changing constantly, Karen, its purpose is to give you a track to follow in the pursuit of your personal goals. As you achieve these steps, replace them with other steps, which will enhance your chances for success. I have written the first two steps down for you—from there on you're on your own." I then handed her the second card. It reads as follows:

Immediate Goals

1. Start aerobics classes next week at (address). The first year has been paid for.

2. Start bringing one sandwich and a piece of fruit to work for lunch. Eat lunch at park across street.

She was momentarily speechless as she read the immediate goal card. I'm sure she was torn between the urge to tell me to "mind my own business," and the desire to thank me for the interest.

When she finally broke the silence, it was with a positive attitude. "Do you mean to tell me that you paid for a year's aerobics for me on the chance that I might follow your advice?"

I answered her question with another question. "Do you want to see your own dreams come true or do you want to be 'little miss perfect secretary' and help to make somebody else's dreams come true?"

She pointed a finger directly at my nose. "You know something Mister, I'm going to take you up on this offer, and I'm going to give it my very best shot, but if I don't make it, I don't want to hear any 'belly-aching' from you."

"You're on," I answered, "we'll say no more about it until I meet you for lunch—in the park—next Thursday."

That was the beginning of an outstanding success story. In our subsequent lunch meetings, I could see her getting noticeably thinner each time we met. In a short time her goals took possession of her actions and she became a different person.

Her story today is a modern Cinderella story. She has an impressive number of weight loss salons; she is well-known for finding new talent through her little theatre work. I have seen her on two recent commercials for national products. Where she will go from here—who knows.

Oh! One more thing. We don't get together very often for lunch anymore. Between her schedule and mine, it's almost impossible. We do talk to each other quite often on the phone however, and we manage to visit one another once or twice during the holidays. I can tell you one thing though. Karen is not apologizing anymore.

If we look closely at Karen's story, we will be able to spot some highly significant probabilities. Foremost in our thoughts should be the very possible outcome of the direction her life was taking. If she had not chosen to take the necessary steps required for the recapturing of her own dreams, perhaps she would still be "the best little secretary in the world," several pounds heavier, with a growing resentment against the mundane mechanics of her occupation. I asked her recently what she thought to be the turning point in her life, aside from the setting of goals.

She replied without hesitation, "I believe the act of 'doing *something*' about my situation eventually opened all the doors." No matter how small the first step had been, the resultant success with that endeavor had strengthened her belief that she could change her life for the better. Her confidence then became the springboard from which she launched each new project, armed with the certainty that she had every right, every probability of success.

There are some people who are fortunate enough to know very early in life what they want to do or become. No question about it, this is a definite plus. It causes them to set a mental goal for where they are heading. Each decision that must be made in their lives is then subconsciously balanced against the quest for this prize. Their success is assured because they have set their heart upon a specific reality.

Unfortunately, those who really don't know what it is they want, are far and away the majority. If we are to "enhance our chances" for success, we must somehow clarify the *direction* in which our goals lie, if not the goals themselves. So many complete their high school education without the foggiest notion of what it is they want to achieve. Still others continue on through college, only to find that the decision has merely been postponed for a few more years, and they still can't decide what it is they want.

I believe the only question that will help to establish the proper goal for you—is this one:

> *What would I like to accomplish, or be, if I could be anything I chose?*

This eliminates the negatives like, "Oh, teachers are in great abundance now, you can't make a decent living at it." Or, "Attorneys are a dime a dozen, maybe you should consider medicine."

The goal that will work best for you is that thing which you **want** to do, not the things that are expedient for the times, or undertaken in an effort to please someone else.

If you're having trouble deciding on a specific goal, then at least decide upon the direction in which your goal lies. If you love horses, and know that your future will have to involve an association with them, get started on a program for learning more about them. Take a job as a groom at some nearby stable. Ask to assist free of charge in the preparation of these handsome animals for your local horse shows. The more involved you become in the "whole" of the picture, the better qualified you will be when you are ready to set that "specific" goal. Somewhere along the road you will decide that you want to be a "rancher," or raise thoroughbreds, or train race horses, or own a riding stable, or become a first-rate trainer.

The goal will present itself to you inevitably, so long as you remain on the road that leads to it.

The same is true of teaching, or medicine, or law, or social work, or engineering, or broadcasting, or whatever. Find the direction in which the desires of your heart lie, and then stay on that path no matter what. The future belongs to those who prepare for it.

There is another subject that should be discussed if we are to "enhance our chances" for success in the attainment of our own personal goals. I'm not a preacher—so the things we are about to discuss will not be approached from a moralistic point of view, or even from a socially acceptable point of view. We will deal instead with "hard facts" as they pertain to the realization of your dreams. Your attitude concerning some of these things may have been established long ago by persons or events from your past and may now be due for an in-depth reevaluation.

But I want you to take a hard look at your chances of success if you have somehow become entangled in a web of "substance addiction," alcoholism, or any of the other "slavemakers."

I'm not your parent, or your parole officer, or your boss, or your husband or wife. I'm your friend. And as such, I am going to level with you right down the line. If you do not have any of the problems we are about to discuss, read this as a warning. Countless persons have struggled up the ladder of success, only to be cut down at the height of their potential by the new-found freedoms, and money that success often brings, when coupled with "bad choices."

Since you and I can talk without getting emotional about it, (a hard thing to ask of parents or other authoritative figures,) let's take our own private look at the facts, and try to determine whether or not there is really cause for concern: My source for the following information is the **U.S. Department of Health and Human Services**. These are the latest available facts:

The implications, trends, and social projections would make a shocking book of considerable length by themselves, but our purpose here is to examine the "known" results as directly as possible in order to allow you to evaluate the probable consequences of involvement without getting mired down in an endless smattering of subject matter.

Marijuana

The strength of today's marijuana is as much as ten times greater than the marijuana used in the 1970s. It can produce a faster heartbeat and pulse rate, bloodshot eyes, and a dry mouth and throat. It does not improve hearing, eyesight, and skin sensitivity as often claimed by its users. It can impair or in some cases practically destroy short-term memory. It can alter the sense of time, and reduce the ability to concentrate. It can affect coordination and swift reaction. It can cause acute "panic anxiety reaction" (the fear of losing control). Long-term users become psychologically addicted and may develop problems with their jobs and personal relationships. Research has shown that the younger people are when they start using marijuana, the more likely they are to go on to other drugs. It can interfere with the learning process by impairing thinking, reading comprehension, and verbal and mathematical skills. Marijuana smoke has been found to be replete with cancer-causing agents; cellular changes called "metaplasia" have been found in the lungs of long-term users. These changes are considered to be *precancerous*. Young people who use marijuana over a long period of time often suffer what is referred to as "burn-out." They become unaware of their surroundings, become dull, slow-moving and inattentive, and strangely, do not seem to be aware that they have a problem. Marijuana users of all ages can arrive at a state where the drug becomes the most important aspect of their lives.

Cocaine

This drug is thought by most recent studies to be "the most addictive of all." In earlier reports, evidence was not available to support that contention, but as the drug became glamorized and popularized by the so-called "jet set," its use has climbed dramatically. Users like the effect it produces and can rapidly arrive at a state where their whole life is centered around seeking and using the drug. It is dependence-producing and some users will go to any lengths to avoid the depression and fatigue they would feel if they stopped using it. Family ties are often broken or severely strained as the user borrows, steals, and even sells items that do not belong to them to support the habit. It can cause a stuffy or runny nose. Chronic snorting can ulcerate the mucous membrane of the nose. Injecting with unsterile equipment can cause hepatitis and other infections. Though few people realize it, overdose deaths can occur when the drug is injected, smoked, or even snorted. Death is caused by multiple seizures followed by respiratory and cardiac arrest.

Hallucinogens and PCP

The effects of psychedelics like LSD are really unpredictable. They vary depending upon the amount taken, the user's personality or mood, and the surroundings in which the drug is taken. Sensations and feelings are often altered, and the user can even feel several different emotions at the same time. Often there is a rapid swing from one emotion to another. The person's sense of time and self change. The sensibilities are often confused, causing the user to believe that they can "hear" colors or "see" sounds. The experience often causes panic. Flashbacks, in which the person does not have to take the drug again, do occur and can be mildly frightening or completely terrifying. Heavy users sometimes develop signs of organic brain damage, impaired memory, reduced attention span, and mental confusion.

PCP effects can vary according to the usage. The immediate results of this drug are: increased heart rate and blood pressure, flushing, sweating, dizziness, and numbness. When large doses are taken, effects include drowsiness, convulsions, and coma. Taking large amounts of PCP can also cause death from repeated convulsions, heart and lung failure, or ruptured blood vessels in the brain.

Inhalants

This is a rather large category, so in the interest of time and space, I will jump to the end results which are highly similar in all inhalants.

The Short-term effects are: loss of self-control, violent behavior, nausea, vomiting, unconsciousness, and loss of touch with one's surroundings.

Sniffing highly concentrated amounts of solvents or aerosol sprays can produce heart failure and instant death. Even on the first try. Long-term use can cause weight loss, fatigue, electrolyte (salt) imbalance, and muscle fatigue. As time progresses, other permanent damage can occur such as irreparable damage to the nervous system, greatly reduced physical and mental capabilities, damage to the liver, kidneys, blood, and bone marrow.

Opiates — Heroin, Etc.

Heroin accounts for 90 percent of the opiate abuse here in the United States. Other drugs are: morphine, meperidine, paragoric, and codeine.

Opiate abusers can develop infections of the heart lining and valves, skin abscesses, and congested lungs. It is common for opiate users to acquire other illnesses through usage of solutions, syringes, and needles. They include liver disease, tetanus, and hepatitis. It is now verifyable fact that pregnant women on these drugs (about 50 percent) suffer anemia, heart disease, diabetes, pneumonia, or hepatitis during pregnancy. They have a high rate of spontaneous abortions, breech deliveries, caesarian sections, premature births, and stillbirths. Infants born to these women often have withdrawal symptoms which may last several weeks or months. Many of these babies die.

Alcohol

This culprit has probably been with us the longest. It's responsible for more misery than all of the other drugs combined. It is without question the leading single cause of death in our nation. Many of the other high-ranking causes of death should rightfully be listed as results occurring from the abuse of this substance. We as a society face a never-ending bombardment of advertising from the media, glorifying the use of alcohol. In 1981 alone, more than 25,000 Americans died in auto accidents caused by drunk drivers. According to a recently released study by "The Bureau Of Justice—Statistics" fifty-four per cent of those convicted of violent crimes had been drinking. The breakdown is frightening.

> 68% of those convicted of manslaughter had been drinking.
> 62% of those convicted of assault had been drinking.
> 49% of those convicted of murder or attempted murder had been drinking.

There are no statistics available concerning the deaths by premature heart attacks, liver disease, and other symptomatic illnesses for which alcohol should rightfully be blamed. It is a drug—it is at the very least, habit forming, and unlike the other drugs it has the full support of the American media, a large segment of the general public, and is sanctimoniously swept under the rug as far as being a health hazard by both the medical profession and our government alike.

The strides I have seen by very small and scattered voices warning of the dangers of alcohol were not made by public officials, men of medicine, or other guardians of our welfare. They were made almost exclusively by courageous individuals who have recognized the danger, suffered as a result of it, or both.

The politicians who have advocated strong steps to curb the danger from drunk drivers, for example, were for the most part jumping on somebody else's bandwagon after they spotted public interest. It is true that recent legislation has now increased the penalties for drunk driving severely in an impressive number of states, but penalties alone won't solve the problem any more than the death penalty solves the problems of murder or rape.

What we have here is a health hazard, and it should be treated as such by all parties concerned. Let there be warnings on the "macho" beer commercials that a great danger exists here. Let there be warnings on the packaging that a threat to your life accompanies the great outdoorsman image the breweries like to project for beer drinkers. We need to **know** our enemies, not to be cajoled into a false sense of "being part of the gang" when our very lives are at risk.

Meanwhile, even as I write, alcohol is a factor in more than half of America's highway deaths. Shouldn't we **do** something about that? How many more of us must lose sons, daughters, wives, or husbands before we make our anger known. I am not blind to the fact that people will continue to drink no matter what is said here or elsewhere, but I don't believe we should go quietly about the task of raising more young people for the gristmill, accepting as unchangeable the fact that we have an **enemy** here, and one who should be portrayed as such while young attitudes are being formed.

We have a right to demand that dangers to the general well-being of the public at large, be made to identify themselves. Even a rattle-snake is required by nature to warn of his presence.

Evaluate

I've no doubt that I will be confronted upon the publication of this book by a number of statements like, "Hey, Rog, I liked your book, but why did you put all that stuff in there about alcohol and drugs?"

We started out to accomplish something here. To examine our attitudes with an eye towards changing our lives for the better. Not everyone who reads this book will have had a spotless record of noninvolvement with some of the things mentioned. They, possibly you, will have to first defeat the enemy that has them prisoner, before moving on to the implementation of the thoughts in this book. Scant reflection should make it obvious to you that there can be no moving forward unless you first face the problem—if you have one.

For those of you who have been victimized by peer pressure, circumstances, social obligation, or the fear of not belonging, I have only this to say: You now know how to examine each new proposition for its truth content. You have the power, now, to pick and choose the things you want to accept or reject. You are entitled to the very best that life has to offer, but the choices are yours. You are at the mercy of no one but yourself. If you are hooked on one of the things we've talked about, do something about it. There is help, but you have to first admit to yourself that there's a problem, and then follow up by reaching out for help.

Remember that hundreds of others have turned their lives around completely. Many of them had problems as great, or greater than yours. You are not alone, although you probably feel at times as though you are. The basic problem has been in your *attitude*. The wrong choices were only symptoms. You can change all that—now.

CHAPTER EIGHT

CHANGING SOCIAL ATTITUDES

There has never been a time in the history of the planet — never — when the forces of both good and evil were so ominously poised to spring at one another — from numberless installations and organizations worldwide — as they are today.

We live in a time of "fearful anticipation" and we search each bit of shocking world news for some clue as to how the conflicting differences could be resolved. We are frustrated by what often appears to be the total abandonment of common sense, rightful disposition, or fair play.

The majority of Americans grew up at a time when we were admired by the rest of the world, and generally perceived to be inventive, ambitious, industrious and, more importantly, free, and right about most of our beliefs. We were the great hope of the world when the legions of Nazi Germany threatened not only Europe, but the rest of the free world as well, and we sacrificed nobly of our blood to defend the rights of many.

We were everybody's darlings, — what happened? I mean what *really* happened. Surely differences in religion, politics, and even national interest could be resolved without bringing the whole of humanity to the brink of destruction? And yet, we view the late news on television with horrified disbelief all too often these days as we witness the thousands of young radical demonstrators at this embassy or that one. In this country or that one, all loudly proclaiming their hatred for — you and I.

Some will search meticulously through the chronicles of political decisions rendered in the past decade or two, in an effort to "fix the blame" for the mess we're in on this administration or that one. Or on one or more of our Presidents. The mistake we seem to repeat over and over again as a conscientious, humanistic society is that of asking ourselves the guilt-producing question "Where did *we* go wrong," or, "How did *we* fail." I think we need to remind ourselves that it is not *"we"* who are bombing embassies around the world. It is not *"we"* who are driving trucks loaded with high explosives into residential areas and detonating them with total lack of concern for the innocent human beings who will be crushed, maimed, and killed in order to make a point for some political faction.

I think the time is now long past due to recognize a very important truth.

We're the good guys!!

And God help the rest of the world if we should ever cease to exist as a major power. But we still need an answer to our question. How did we go from darling of the world to "hated imperialistic, capitalistic America"?

The truth is — **we stand in the way of evil**, and from that position we will constantly and ruthlessly be under assault from the forces of darkness. Does that sound bizarre to you? Well, consider this line from the Bible.

> *For we wrestle not against flesh and blood, but against principalities, against powers, against the rulers of the darkness of this world, against spiritual wickedness in high places.*

> *Ephesians Chapter 6*
> *Verse 12.*

We have a right as Americans to be extremely proud of the role that God has chosen for us to play in the affairs of men and of nations. Our attitude concerning our country should be one of humble gratitude, fierce loyalty, and constant vigilance. Let's put to rest once and for all the absurd notion that we are the oppressors of other nations.

A short study of the actions of certain other world leaders such as the Ayatollah Khomeini of Iran, or Khadafy of Libya, will disclose quite vividly that *their* attitudes toward even their own countrymen who don't happen to agree with them, is one of barbarous, murderous vengeance.

Nations that have nothing to offer their citizens save poverty and bloodshed take great delight in creating a scapegoat to blame their troubles upon. It takes the focus of attention off of *them*, and places it instead upon some invented enemy.

The hatred that gushes forth from the leadership of most Marxist-inspired countries sets man against the rationale of his own conscience, and moves him to lash out heartlessly in acts of senseless terrorism and brutal, indiscriminate destruction of life and property.

Although we hear about some of these mind-boggling, inhuman acts, those that happen to catch the attention of the media, the average American has no idea how widespread is this policy of "killing for emphasis." Joe Poyer, military consultant in guerilla warfare and field editor for *International Combat Arms magazine*, was recently quoted as stating, "Since 1982 there have been more than 400 terrorist acts yearly."

Whether it's the Shiite Moslems of Lebanon, or the crazed gunmen of El Salvador who recently sprayed an outdoor cafe with machine gun fire killing 13 people, including four Americans, the trademark remains the same.

Hatred and death, are the calling cards of the other great alliance in the world.

You do not see people waiting for years, by the hundreds of thousands, to get into any of those other countries as they have been doing here for as long as we can remember.

I think it should be totally clear by now to anyone who has the common sense to add up the events of the past 40 years or so that it is *"we"* who are in the right. Please don't hand me any of that garbage about how our policies of the past have created all of these difficult problems, for all of these little countries. If you've "bought" that fairy tale, then I believe you should do a complete examination of the facts on your own.

There's something else.

I am convinced that the real battle is between good and evil, and I believe that the battle lines are even now being drawn. You may one day soon have to decide upon which camp you will serve. Reluctantly, I can only interpret the constantly escalating arms race and the brainless acts of terrorism by puppet governments as preludes to a far greater conflict. There is, however, hope . And it rests not in the strength of our armed might (although I am a strong believer in being prepared) but rather in the greatest all-out attack that has ever been undertaken, for the hearts of men.

The *attitude* of the common man is the one great power that can change the suicidal course that we are all now embarked upon.

I'm delighted when I see news of religious organizations penetrating areas that were once forbidden to them. I'm thrilled when I see steps being taken to *educate* people who never had that advantage before.

It's hard to lead learned people to commit acts of wanton violence against the innocent. It's easy to get large armies of those who have known nothing but poverty and ignorance to follow you — if you will feed them and give them power (a gun). The Soviet block has been exploiting that situation for many years. Some years ago, someone coined a clever little phrase that struck right to the heart of our deepest fears. If I recall correctly, it went something like this: *"Wouldn't it be great if they gave a war and nobody came?"* What a great goal that would be. To have the common people of all nations of one mind, heart, and attitude. For any hint of conflict, made by the leaders of the world, to be met by incredulous stares of disbelief, and a flat refusal to participate.

The key, of course, would have to be a *"universal"* denunciation of war as a means for acquiring goals. What steps could be taken to assure all parties concerned that they would not be denouncing war, only to be annihilated by other nations that were not so peacefully inclined?

There would have to be an international organization of great strength, composed of the common people of all nations, aligned with **no** other political goals or aspirations. The one and only common thread that would bind this great worldwide movement would be the quest for—a world without war.

Every race, religion, political persuasion, and people would be welcome so long as they left their other interests, to be dealt with in other arenas.

It has been predicted that mankind will one day "beat his swords into plowshares and study war no more." I believe the time to begin that project in earnest—is now.

If we were to pursue a course dedicated to the absence of war, what steps could we take to begin the process? How could we plant the seeds of mutual survival in the hearts of the world's citizens, and what exactly have we got going for us at this point that would aid in this gigantic undertaking?

Well, the good news is—we really don't have to be concerned with waking people up to the fact that humanity is threatened. They already know that, and most are just as concerned as you and I. So we needn't be worried about "selling" the benefits of our program. We already have a worldwide audience—waiting for answers.

I am of the opinion that our very first step should be to realize we are dealing with a *"spiritual"* problem here, not a political one. And that therefore, we need to establish the *attitude* we will take as we press on. Of necessity, we will have to embrace all who support our cause as brothers and sisters equally and purge from our thoughts anything judgemental about other areas of their lives. It would require a devotion to the singular purpose of life without war, resisting along the way all attempts at encroachment by any other interest. Adding other causes to the quest, no matter how pure or honorable they might appear to be, would only serve to dilute the spirit of the movement.

You may wonder why I view this great universal hunger as belonging in the realm of the spirit, rather than in politics or some other national interest. I'll try to explain.

I believe that the desire for world peace — the absence of war — has been one of the fundamental cravings of the soul ever since the first angry man picked up a club and allowed himself to be overwhelmed by the evil urge to do harm to his brother. I'm persuaded as well that the so-called "winners" of modern day gargantuan clashes between men and machinery pay a price far too terrible to allow any heartfelt joy in the victory.

Every war of nations has left hundreds of thousands of innocents standing on the sidelines, grieving their hearts out for a dear face that would never again be seen. For every young warrior who has fallen in battle, on *both* sides of the conflict, a hundred lives are altered sadly, profoundly, and forever.

Other than for self-preservation, is there a goal in war really worth the ghastly price? Aside from the control of our own lives, our freedoms, and the inviolable sanctity of our nation, what can be worth the horrible cost? Dwight D. Eisenhower once said that "war is the pursuance of political aims." He was right of course, but I put it to you. Is any political aim worth the great, grey ghost of grief that blankets the world like ripples spreading ever wider from the point of disturbance on a clear, calm pond? And yet, small angry bands of men in a hundred nations flirt dangerously with the sparks of worldwide flame. Each professes in their own way to be searching for peace — radical provocation is *not* the path to peace — but they will beat that drum loudly, because it's the only one they have. And yet — and yet — there truly beats within their heart that ever-present longing to raise their families without fear.

The ubiquitous spirit that has settled upon mankind because of the horrible spectre of a thermonuclear holocaust is now ripe for expression. When millions of souls pray and long for a single happening in the affairs of men, that dream far transcends the smallness of individual goals, political or otherwise, and becomes a common spiritual bond with a strength and momentum all its own.

I don't mean to suggest even for a moment that we have the answer to world peace here, but I do believe that the time is ripe for peace-loving people all over the world to make their presence known. The hour is late, yet nothing succeeds like an idea whose time has come. Perhaps we can serve to notify all nations that in the quest for peace — we're with you.

We must all stand and say, "I will have no part in the killing of innocent men, women, and children. Find some other way to resolve your differences, gentlemen. This has now become a war against evil, and we will search for ways to combat evil. If we destroy millions of innocents in the process, we will in fact be *serving* that evil."

There can be no greater victory for the forces of darkness than all-out carnage, dressed in the cloak of righteousness. All sides are convinced that their cause is just. The leadership of every nation feeds the populace a well-planned diet of national indignation, stressing of course the uprightness of their endeavors and maligning — with little thought as to the reciprocal fruits of that act — the motives of the opposition.

Love of homeland then becomes the weapon whereby great armies are assembled in support of all manner of half-understood objectives, and countless millions go marching off to destroy, and to be destroyed with the sound of patriotism ringing loudly in their ears.

We need to question loud and long the full reasons behind any attempt to mobilize man against man. And I mean **all** Nations. I want to elucidate so there can be no misunderstanding.

Just as we learned in an earlier chapter to "question" our former indoctrination, we must insist, as citizens of a world grown much too small for conflict, that all the facts in any contested issue be made known to the people involved. The old stance of "It's best that they don't know" is now totally outdated. Just as war is now outdated.

The rules must somehow be made to apply to all nations. The apocalyptic nature of recent events *demands* that the citizens of **each** nation take a far more active role in the conduct of their respective countries than that of electing, appointing, or accepting without question the mandates of the few in power.

If we are to change the status quo, the loudest voices of every nation must be those of its citizens. It is no longer acceptable for the elite few to make decisions of life or death for millions of people who are for the most part ignorant of the true reasons for those decisions.

Anyone who has spent time in countries other than their own, knows full well that "people are people the world over," and that the desire for peace is universal. If the enemy is not really "other people," then we need to know and to define the nature of this enemy so that we may better prepare to defend ourselves and to bring appropriate weapons in to play against this elusive ghost, while there is yet time.

I'll repeat myself. *"The enemy is evil itself,"* and the leaders are "the rulers of the darkness of this world and spiritual wickedness in high places." What are the traits of this evil, and how do we begin to counteract its devastating influence? Here are some of the weapons and areas of exploitation utilized by the enemy.

Hunger, poverty, lack of knowledge, spiritual suppression, limited access to information, a diet of hate against appointed enemies (starting with the very young,) promotion and increased status for those who carry out orders blindly (without questioning their morality,) a cold disinterest in the horror and suffering caused innocent people by senseless acts of violence.

There are others of course, but one need only read the newspapers for a day or two in order to confirm the constant existence of operatives of this ruthless camp.

Now, remembering that we are engaged in a *"spiritual"* battle here, what weapons do we have at **our** disposal? Are we defenseless? Must we battle on 'til the end of time with no hope for the dignity of man to overcome at last the darkness of ignorance?

I'm afraid that question has yet to be answered. Will the "goodness" of man in the end be strong enough to set aright the terrible injustices that have spawned and nurtured the evil giant that now threatens us all? I hope so — no, I pray so.

I'm sure of one thing. We need to stop apathetically accepting as unchangeable the present course we are on, and we need to unite spiritually in an optimistic, determined expedition to "pull the teeth" of mankind's common enemy — **war.**

On the bright side, there has never been a time in history when it has been easier to get information into the hands of the great masses of the world's peoples than it is today. In our own great nation, the news media is constantly probing and prodding in a never-ending search for truth, and I say " Thank God for that." Granted, they get carried away on occasion and "invite conclusion" here and there, but by and large they do a tremendous job.

What we need to encourage, is this same type of access to truth in all the nations of the world. Our best hope for combating darkness — is light. For neutralizing lies — truth. We need also to encourage in every nation the free exchange of products and goods, the selfless sharing of ideas, technology, know-how, education, and spiritual freedom. Instead of armed camps that do not know or trust each other, we need a world of good neighbors dedicated to the pursuit of peaceful goals and reciprocal trust. This can only take place when great peoples of the world **demand** that the barriers to the free exchange of information and the monolithic stance of the super-powers be toppled. Let us run across the borders both geographical and psychological to embrace one another, to proclaim loudly, "Long live your children — and mine." We have thrown our weapons into the dust. We have denounced forever the horrors of Hades with which we once sought to cow the spirit of one another. We have learned at last that we will reap what we sow. That threat of annihilation produces threat of annihilation. We have grasped hands firmly and I have looked searchingly into your eyes. I could find no enemy there, only a man like myself. But with that touching of spirits came the awful discovery that we both alike had been duped. That a force of great maniacal power had screamed hoarsely at us from a thousand battle fields to hate, to kill, to perceive one another as less than human. And in that moment of pure and absolute truth, we saw together, you and I, the face of our real enemy. The fallen one — the great manipulator. And we saw clearly for the very first time the true prizes for which the countless battles had really been fought. We shuddered together in fear as we witnessed the awesome harvest — of the souls of men.

It has often been stated, in one way or another, and by authorities far too numerous to mention, that where good men fail to act, evil prospers. Perhaps we're suffering some of the long-term results of our own apathy. Although we have always been a generous nation, and Americans can always be counted upon to help out the less fortunate in times of crisis, I wonder if as a national policy we have been too lax in assisting poor countries on a day-to-day basis. An empty stomach is certainly fertile ground in which to stir the passions of hatred. Perhaps we should do less preaching and more feeding. Who wants to listen to speeches about Democracy when their stomach is growling? Have we allowed our pride for our country and way of life to blind us to the *real* needs of our neighbors? Maybe we have the cart before the horse. Maybe we should first see to it that no one goes hungry — and **then** we'll discuss Democracy — on a full stomach.

In some of the Latin American countries, we are now pouring millions of dollars in military aid into their coffers. Wouldn't it have been wiser to be "the good big brother to the North" when they were trying to build their national economies? Now we find ourselves in competition for the loyalties of their peoples, and we're developing an ever more potent case of paranoia about communist influence in South America. I question seriously whether there could have been any valid threat against the U.S. had we been on hand to help all these years. And I don't mean "token help in exchange for political favors."

In an earlier chapter I made reference to the fact that we are indeed our brother's keepers. I believe that applies equally to our responsibility as a great nation and the leader of the free world. Of whom much is given, much is expected. Perhaps we should practice a bit more "preventive maintenance." It's far better to be deeply involved in business, farming, and other fruitful endeavors with a nation than it is to be arming half of the populace, to defend itself against the other half. The point is — we may be contributing to our own political difficulties by failing to meet our responsibilities as a great nation.

The other negative reality that has often been exploited by governments hostile to our own, is ignorance. The lack of formal education. You can easily control large blocks of the world's people by the mere act of providing them with three important basics that very nearly every person alive craves to some extent. They are: Food — Power — A cause (or purpose.)

Imagine if you will, that you are witness to the simple life style of a small South American village. It really doesn't matter much in which country these scenes take place. The setting is an oft-repeated one, polished to perfection over a period of time by the cadres of "contrived revolution."

The first apparent common denominator, you will note, is the almost pathetic poverty in which the inhabitants of the village spend their lives. If you've never before been out of the United States, the culture shock, as you realize that millions of the earth's people do indeed go to bed hungry at night, can be quite overwhelming. There is a drabness and a sameness about the routines of the men who work long, hard hours in the hot South American sun just to keep food on the table. The women also suffer long, backbreaking hours of toil in an attempt to earn the few more pesos that might provide clothing for the little ones. The fact that one has been "born into" this kind of squalor does **not** make it more palatable. The people who must live out their lives in hopeless forbearance are just as discontented as you or I would be.

They long for the things that others can afford. Shoes for the children, pretty dresses for the little girls, a bright new sombrero for the handsome young son. But the bottom rung of the social ladder, that of the field worker, offers little hope, little chance, for those luxuries.

And then one day, a note is tacked to the huge wooden door on the village church. It is read aloud by a village elder in slow, deliberate speech.

The note speaks of opportunity, of changes to come that will alter forever the nature of their lives. And it asks for their help, for their faith in a cause. It implores them to come to a meeting at the church, tonight.

As the sun's last remaining oranges and reds begin to fade, from the onset of night, and the smoke of a hundred small cooking fires, the villagers walk slowly toward the little church, with muted hope in their hearts and a quickening pulse for the promise, the short but forceful note seemed to hold.

They are met outside the church by an impressive sight. There are eight men dressed in sharp, neatly fitting uniforms, assembled on a slightly raised wooden platform which seems to have appeared as if out of nowhere.

Six of the men carry automatic weapons at the ready position, their black berets cocked jauntily to one side, their wide smiles looking strangely out of place in this setting. The other two men appear to be officers, and are busily engaged in looking over printed matter at the hastily assembled speaker's podium located front and center of the platform.

When at last the few remaining stragglers from points beyond the confines of the village have arrived, the eldest of the two men smiles broadly and begins to speak. His attitude, in spite of the six armed men on his flanks, is one of humility and supplication. He talks about "national honor," about his great love for his country, about the need for sweeping changes. His entire speech is peppered with references to the horrible conditions his "fellow patriots" are forced to endure. He draws vivid word pictures of the unjust advantages enjoyed by certain elements close to, and favored by the present regime. He fans the flame of discontent with pointed reminders of the poverty, and hopeless condition, and the lack of pride that his listeners, their children, and their childrens' children shall forever be forced to suffer—unless **"we"** rise up together as the true patriots of the nation and stand tall and strong until the last survivors of the oppressive regime have been driven into the sea.

The conclusion to this speech is marked by tears and by a moving appeal to his "fellow countrymen" to join him in this sacred pilgrimage. He then seats himself, reverently resting his forehead in his hand.

The second orator is not so restrained, or humble. He is a younger, powerfully built man with a strong, authoritative manner and a booming voice that can easily be heard by the furthermost persons in attendance.

He quotes fact and figure concerning everything from food allotment, to per capita earnings by district. He enumerates the sins of the current regime in loud, accusatory tones. And at last he booms out the "guilt by association" theme, condemning the present leadership of the nation for its "Yankee imperialist leanings." There follows then a fullblown attack on the actions and motives of the United States. **We** become the target. The behind-the-scenes culprit responsible for all of their troubles.

It may all seem somewhat crude to you, but it's effective. On the heels of this beginning, the young men are recruited into the military, given training, given weapons, and fired up almost daily with large doses of anti-American hate speeches. In addition to that, many of these youngsters are, for the first time in their lives, eating regularly.

Can we blame them? Can we honestly blame these people for grasping at any straw that comes their way offering an "out" from the life they have been forced to lead? Wouldn't we do the same? As unpleasant as all of this is to hear, I hope it will serve to underscore for you the simplicity with which formidable armies can be raised in our own backyard and perhaps illustrate the necessity for providing alternatives for the poor and oppressed of the world.

It should be noted that rarely, (if ever) do these new regimes deliver what they purport to represent. Historically, they create yet more problems for a nation by syphoning off the young people and leaving the old to manage without them. Moreover, the young who have tasted the strong ale of power are highly unlikely to return to the subserviant ways of their fathers.

There is an answer, but it's late in coming. We have to create a world in which there is **no need** to raise up armies. The technology exists — now — to solve the problems of hunger, poverty, ignorance, personal freedom, religious persecution and the like. But the world has become so mesmerized by the mistaken belief that awsome military power can somehow solve the areas of disagreement between nations, that we have in fact lost sight of the true *nature* of our problems. We can compare the position of world powers to that of a young lad at the beach, trying to build a sand-castle with one hand, while fighting off the destructive tendencies of other youngsters with the other hand. What sand-castles we could build together, if both hands were free for the building.

Let's begin by erasing some of the old conceptions. We need to think about the *positive* aspects of a world grown weary of war. I sense a very vibrant, energetic movement in opposition to anything that smacks of destruction. It's growing quietly now in many places, under many names, but it is dynamic in nature and it is worldwide. There are organizations of formidable wealth and influence who have visualized the conquest of man over his destructive tendencies, taken some of the steps necessary to initiate improved understanding, cultural exchanges, and the free flow of information so vital to the survival of any new alliance where the participants had formerly perceived one another with great suspicion.

We're not talking about a simple task — I think we all realize that. But we're not talking about an impossible one either. Not so many years ago we saw China as an enemy. She was not brought to her knees by our military might, she was not intimidated by our destructive capabilities; she was, in the end persuaded that it was in the best interest of the Chinese people to do business with the U.S. and to build bridges of friendship between the two nations. The results to date have been beneficial to all concerned.

We now have a new and growing market for our products and services. China now has a new source of expertise in many areas, unavailable to her in the past. The same can be said of Japan, or West Germany. We see them now as friends and trade partners (even though we have our little family squabbles.)

The more you get to know your neighbor, the less likely you are to quarrel with him about who gets the fruit from a tree which overlaps both properties. Especially if you just enjoyed a barbeque at his house.

We need to build those bridges. The world has become too small a neighborhood for war.

Our technological capability has been outstripping our intellectual progression. It's time to move up to a higher plateau. To throw away the toys of war, and to concentrate now on the other serious problems that beset mankind. We have not, as a world society of many peoples, come of age as yet. But the time to grow up was never better than it is right now. The sick and the poor, the hopeless and the lost, they all cry out for our maturity. The two great camps of outlook, of spiritual attitude, are this day aligning themselves for the battle to claim the loyalties of men.

Both have shown boldness of action above and beyond anything that has been seen in the past. On the one side we see hijackings, random killings, indiscriminate bombings, and a total lack of concern for innocent bystanders. On the other, we can feel that same energetic, positive spirit I spoke of earlier. We are witnessing history at its finest when we see massive shows, composed of the finest talent the world has to offer in the field of modern entertainment, all brought together for the singular purpose of raising money to feed the starving people of the world. That's the way we *should* be dealing with the problems that confront mankind. Organized, together, determined, and without bothering to inquire as to which side of the political fence the recipients are on.

Again, during the 1984 Olympics, millions of people around the world were moved to tears as they watched the finest athletes humanity has to offer, join hands in a magnificent display of spiritual unity as they sang together of reaching out, of touching, and of making the world a better place.

The mutual respect and honor shown to, as well as by, the individual athletes at that great festival of nations could well serve as a model for other areas of international competition. Let's be willing to help one another at every opportunity, so that a victory for one, is in fact a victory for all. When we have learned **that** lesson, we will at last be ready to stand together as one family and to renounce forever the absurdities of "power posturing" and automatic condemnation of the unfamiliar.

There can be no unity of purpose, no true revelation of man's *real* enemies until we are willing to accept the whole of mankind as part of the family. Once having done that, we will wisely begin to search out, and focus our attention upon the *real* motivators of man's discontent. I must warn you . The season that lies directly ahead will be one of violent actions on many fronts. The evil one knows his days are numbered, and he will for that reason thrash wildly about, setting man against man in as many places as possible. But the attitudes of men are changing. They're winning the battle against ignorance. They're recognizing one another as brothers, and they are not quite so willing to go charging off to war for the dubious honors of soldiering as they once might have been.

There will also be frequent and ever-escalating attacks against religion. Man's faith keeps him in touch with the inborn knowledge of good and evil. These things will be ridiculed, laughed at, and the things of the spirit will not be believed by many. Perhaps even now, this whole section of the book sounds strangely unbelievable to you. I hope not. If we can be deceived into believing that the spirit is dead or nonexistent, it won't be long before we will begin to rationalize every act we choose to commit on the basis of "what's in it for me" or "the end justifies the means" or some other self-indulgent attitude which has been stripped bare of the soundness and everlasting endurance that comes only with those things that are rooted in the spiritual side to man's unique and favored relationship with his God.

Although I have striven to avoid sermonizing in these pages, it is next to impossible to probe honestly into the conduct of men and nations without tripping repeatedly over the errors, and violations of ancient taboos which were established dramatically, unforgetably, so that man might live in harmony with man, and prosper in the peaceful pursuit of happiness alongside his loved ones.

In the end—will it be as the sages have told us? Is the real cause of our difficulties, our long separation from our creator, and the exploitation of that condition by the fallen angel? Probably. What better reason then to see to our attitudes. To examine closely our long held beliefs about other peoples, and to test those beliefs, no matter where we learned them, against the expanded knowledge that time and experience has given us.

Do we really have any room in the world for prejudice? Has the act of belittling a people, or condemning a class, or suppressing a race ever achieved one single solitary thing? No—nor shall it ever.

My Country Right or Wrong

Within the confines of the United States of America, there has been assembled during the last two hundred plus years, the greatest aggregation of diverse religions, philosophies, races of people, and individual seekers of freedom from every imaginable background that has ever gathered under one national roof.

This bold and unheard of experiment was made workable by the common cement of "tolerance." In 1917 a man named William Tyler Page of Maryland won a nationwide contest for the best summary of the political faith of America. His piece was entitled *"Americans Creed,"* and although he borrowed lines from other famous American documents, I find his perception of our national political fibre as appropriate today as it was when he wrote it. It reads as follows:

> *I believe in the United States of America as a government of the people, by the people, for the people; whose just powers are derived from the consent of the governed; a democracy in a republic; a sovereign Nation of many sovereign States; a perfect Union, one and inseparable; established upon those principles of freedom, equality, justice, and humanity for which American patriots sacrificed their lives and fortunes. I therefore believe it is my duty to my country to love it; to support its Constitution; to obey its laws; to respect its flag; and to defend it against all enemies.*
>
> *William Tyler Page*

The bedrock principles upon which our nation was founded are known to all of us. Lesser known, however, are the responsibilities that each of us should shoulder on a day-to-day basis in order to preserve the Union and the calibre of its people. Our early patriots were for the most part men of God. The wisdom of our founding Fathers has come to be admired by all nations of the world, not because of their victories in battle over the well-trained British regulars, but because of the strange new concept of a government that would function as "servant to the people" instead of the other way 'round. Such a government, in order to survive, would have to contain concerned citizens who would monitor the movements of the governing body closely, and who would stand up boldly to denounce those actions that were not in harmony with the spirit of the Republic. We have fortunately, always had men and women who were willing to do just that. But I want to discuss with you my concern about some other areas of the American dream that seem to have lost their significance in the eyes of some of our citizens as the years have flown by.

Mr. Page, in the last line of his Creed, speaks of defending the Nation against all enemies. I take this to mean the small, insidious inroads against the moral fiber of our people as well as for the more obvious military threats from without.

The unparalleled freedom that Americans had won when our nation was young used to be accompanied by a strong, almost religious determination by our forefathers to be the very best that they could be in whatever walk of life they had chosen for themselves. We were, in the beginning, a proud people, a productive people, and we remained that way for many years.

At an earlier point in his book we talked about the changes that had occurred following World War II. I would like to pursue that subject a bit further in order to explore with you some possible areas in which we could stand improvement. Thank God for the privilege that you and I have of living in a nation where we can "speak our mind" without fear of death or prison. May we never lose that. It is, after all, one of the cornerstones of personal freedom upon which this nation was founded.

Should that right be taken from us, it will mean that we did not use it often enough, and that we stood mutely by while our freedoms were eroded away before our very eyes. Whoever said, *"The price of freedom is eternal vigilance,"* certainly knew what he was talking about.

I see a subtle danger to our nation in the form of certain *national attitudes*. I fear that we have permitted some rather inaccurate interpretations of our freedoms to jeopardize, or at least to "chip away at" the rights of other segments of our society.

The precious right to "stand tall wherever you will" ceases to be a right when you are standing on somebody else's foot. Freedom is our inherent right in this nation unless, or until our freedom curtails the rights of one of our fellow citizens. It then becomes a violation of the whole spirit of freedom and equality.

In the quest for the American dream we seem to have somehow confused our priorities to the point that "financial gain" has taken precedent over pride in workmanship, professional integrity, and even moral obligation. Some of our citizens have suffered, as the result of this twisting of proper attitudes and continue to pay a heavy price for the inevitable results.

Automobile manufacturers, for example, had a marvelous heyday following World War II, and for a period of approximately twenty-five years, with the exception of a couple of recession years, and until the foreign car manufacturers began to make serious inroads with the American consumer.

How were Japan and other nations able to capture so easily, sizeable chunks of the American market? Easy. While we were throwing chrome and gadgets on our cars and fighting constantly along the way for higher wages (through the unions,) Japan was making cars that were smaller, more fuel efficient, more dependable, and would last longer — and selling them cheaper. In other words, they were building quality cars which reflected pride in the workmanship, and selling them at a fair price. We, on the other hand, were clamoring for more money through the unions and then passing the cost on to the consumers, who were of course our fellow Americans. Furthermore, the quality of American made cars began to suffer — some of you will remember the many newspaper articles. It never should have happened that way, but we allowed our greed to cost us a staggering portion of our gross national product which we may now never recover. The loss in jobs and income was inestimable.

Then there's the medical profession, in particular as it relates to the older, retired citizens of our nation. We Americans have revered our medical practitioners almost to the point of "blind, submissive compliance" not only to methods of treatment and health maintenance, but beyond that also to the passionless acceptance of ridiculous charges far in excess of reasonable billing practices. The very nature of the medical profession seems somehow to inhibit our willingness to demand that our doctors abide by the same rules of "fair trade practices" that we require of other professions.

I'm well aware of the old adage, " When your health is at stake, money is no object," but I don't believe that should be interpreted to mean, "When you need medical advice or treatment, pay any price without complaint."

We have viewed the problem with a "witch-doctor" mentality, as if to suggest that the act of calling on doctors and hospitals to account for their financial ethics from time to time would somehow imperil our health.

The high esteem with which we regard our practitioners, along with an almost reverent respect for anyone associated with the saving or mending of lives, has stigmatized realistic perception of the problem.

It needs to be said:
> **Doctors and hospitals charge far too much for
> their services.**

Having said that, let's examine together the impact upon another segment of our society — the retired — as a direct result of these staggering medical bills. In 1974 the total health care costs for people 65 and over were approximately 24 billion dollars.

Ten years later, in 1984, that figure had soared to an astonishing 120 billion dollars. More than half of that was **not** paid by Medicare. Simple calculation will show you that what Medicare won't pay today is over 2½ times the total health care costs of only ten years ago. Obviously something is drastically wrong. The U.S. Department of Labor's *Bureau of Labor Statistics* (CPI detailed report, 1984) informs us that hospital costs alone have risen a whopping 86 percent during the past five years.

Now, what options are available to retired people on a fixed income to cope with the problem, and how does this national dilemma affect the rest of us?

The primary defense against the ballooning portion of medical bills not covered by Medicare is the purchase of "Medicare

Supplement" insurance. The companies that write this type of coverage are for the most part in a constant state of change, endlessly revamping their respective programs in an effort to cope with the ever-escalating portion of bills which do not qualify for Medicare benefits. Unfortunately, this means they must also charge additional premiums for their products.

In recent years many former owners of this type of coverage have opted instead to discontinue the purchase of Medicare Supplement insurance and to apply for financial aid from the various "State" agencies.

Whether paying a higher premium for insurance or throwing themselves upon the mercy of state-administered programs, the retired senior is reacting, in the vast majority of cases, to a pressure situation which realistically threatens to "wipe out" the accumulated savings of a lifetime.

I believe this to be one of the most serious problems that our retired citizens are faced with. Moreover, the cost of state-run programs and the "spread" of higher insurance premiums is born by the rest of our society and will continue to be paid for as the price tag increases, by our children, and our children's children. We can begin to grasp the gargantuan size of this developing monster when we realize that in addition to the 25 million Americans who are already over age 65, their number grows by an unbelievable 5,000 new retirees **every single day**. They are the fastest-growing age group in the nation.

What these figures say to me is this: Doctors, hospitals, and all health-related services and supplies, from X-rays to aspirin, from anesthesia to "stand-by physicians" (that's the guy you get a bill from following surgery, who you never heard of) are completely out of line with their charges. Although I'm aware that the day of the family doctor who was willing to accept anything from a live chicken to a bag full of apples for his services has long since passed, I cannot buy the concept that the years of study required to become a physician or some other medical professional, automatically grants license to charge exorbitant prices far above and beyond a *fair* price for services rendered.

When greed replaces fair play in a nation, and that situation is allowed to continue unchecked, there will be a national price to pay and we will all suffer for it.

Look about you at some of our fellow citizens who are in trouble today and then backtrack to the recent history of that group. Very often you'll find that a few years ago, these people were at the top of the list in earnings and job security — but still demanding more. The greed of a nation bent upon success at any price, eventually necessitates the seeking of alternatives by those who are victimized. That's why we have American auto manufacturers who are now building their cars in foreign countries. That's why steel to build American products comes from foreign shores. And who pays the price for the resultant loss of jobs and income? We all do, but the American wage earner suffers the most.

Perhaps we have reached a point in our history when we should begin to value fairness above immediate gain. Maybe the time has come to return to the principles of our fathers and to look with suspicion upon the loud voices who promise more of everything, yet in the end, cause us to lose that which we already had.

We are a nation that needs to reevaluate who we are, and what we stand for. Deplorably, the passing of time has caused us to fix new priorities and to abandon — to some extent — the true spirit of freedom of which we were born. What genius of evil have we permitted to rob us of our inborn sense of justice, our pride of self and purpose.

At what point in time did we trade off "In God we trust" for "Success at any price"?

The mindless pursuit of dollars has not been confined to any *one* profession or occupation. It has, in fact, evolved into a way of life for millions of Americans, notably the young. Have we abdicated our responsibilities to our children to teach them of the truly valuable things in life?

Have we, by the mere act of stressing financial success, relegated to second position the ingredients of strong and noble character?

These are questions we all need to ask ourselves. The attitude with which the upcoming generation confronts problems of national and international direction will most certainly touch the lives of us all.

Perhaps now is the time for the aristocracy of our spiritual leadership to step forward boldly and pronounce again and again the truisms of human value. Dr. Charles H. Malik of Lebanon, while attending a major review conference of the United Nations (June 23 through June 26, 1985, at San Francisco) made the following comments:

> *"It is to the spirit and mind of man, to his ideas and his attitudes, that we must devote considerable attention if the peace is going to be truly won. Unless we secure the right conditions for spiritual and intellectual health and unless we determine the right positive ideas for which man should live, I am afraid all our work in this conference may prove to have been in vain."*

Leaders from every corner of the globe are beginning to recognize that the framework of any truly lasting agreement among men, cannot be achieved until the attitudes of the participants can produce a meeting of the spirit. Diverse national goals will always be a formidable challenge. As U.S. Secretary of State Shultz remarked while reviewing the past 40 years of the United Nations:

> *"Divisions among nations and peoples persisted so that we continue to live in a world of sovereign nations, of competing interests and clashing philosophies."*

The *attitudes* of our future leaders will be the key ingredients which may one day penetrate the foggy, slippery, iron-cased barriers that befuddle the efforts of man. And that, not until we recognize in spirit, our common enemy, "the adversary of all mankind," "the spirit who now works in the sons of disobedience." (Eph. 2:2.)

In Defense Of Excellence

We, who live in the world today, are the unwilling victims of our time. Since 1945 and the end of World War II, there have been 154 conventional wars, affecting 71 countries and resulting in twenty million casualties. This is the aftermath — mind you — of the second great war to end all wars.

The industrial revolution, in addition to changing the face of the earth forever, brought with it the tempting illusion that a nation capable of mass-producing machines of horrendous destructive power could, in fact, rule the world. Alfred Krupp (1812-1887) of Germany perfected a method of casting steel cannon which helped Prussia defeat Austria in 1866, and France in 1870. (Few people remember that he also developed the first seamless railway wheel, a remarkable achievement at the time.) It had been demonstrated that great weapons could produce great victories, or so they thought. And the Krupp works eventually became "Krupp Munitions." In two world wars Germany unleashed massive assaults of men and machines against her European neighbors. Hitler was fascinated by the awesome power of the war machines, and along with his generals developed the now famous "Blitzkrieg." The word means "lightning war" and for a time in the early days of World War II, the dreaded Panzer Tank divisions, other mechanized units, and German dive-bombers raced across most of Europe without serious opposition. German steel ruthlessly crushed the life from all resistance, and the blood of patriots defending their respective homelands reddened the soil of many nations.

Hitler had, by this time, totally bought the concept that Germany could rule the world. But the most disturbing development of all was what followed next. The German people, that intelligent, industrious, inventive race began to believe that they actually were a super-race. They allowed themselves to be carried along by the ravings of the power-mad Fuhrer, and thus a *"national attitude"* was established, paving the way for unspeakable horrors against the whole of humanity.

If you have watched the old movie newsreels of that period, you will remember the two faces of Hitler. He is generally remembered as a forceful orator, raging against those whom he considered to be enemies of the Third Reich. The other picture we have of him is that of a jubilant leader, laughing with his generals as he adds yet another notch to his gun in the shootout of nations.

What I want you to search your memory for is not the face of Hitler, but rather, the faces of the great throngs of German people to whom he was speaking. They were not, as many suppose, a nation of captives, led down the path of world war against their will. They were in fact for the most part, devoted to the Fuhrer and hung upon his every word with childlike anticipation.

The great "Sieg Heil" salutes were not reluctantly given in mechanical fashion. They were enthusiastically and forcefully shouted in genuine support and allegiance for their leader. Even today, forty years later, those of us who heard those salutes can easily hear them again, ringing across our memories. "Sieg Heil"—"Sieg Heil"—"Sieg Heil." And the polished boots of the mighty war machine marched obediently off to trample into the dust any resistance against the master race.

It has to be one of the most unbelievable occurrances of the 20th century. That a gifted people like the Germans could allow themselves to be so misled by a dream of power that they would follow blindly the shouting, strutting dictator, Adolph Hitler. There were of course a great many circumstances favorable to his rise to power at that time, but the sheer incongruity of a nation which had given the world countless intellectuals, philosophers, musicians, artists, playwrights, poets, and other great thinkers is almost beyond comprehension.

There are at least two very frightening legacies that we've inherited from those evil days.

One: The early successes of the Nazi war machine continue to haunt us on many fronts today as certain nations and factions relentlessly pursue a course of intimidation by military force, having learned nothing from the defeat of Nazi Germany.

Two: So long as we do not recognize evil and speak out against it, there will be fertile ground for the rise of demonic leaders who can pervert the attitudes of a nation.

We absolutely must face the truth. There is no military machine, no superweapon, no amount of hydrogen bombs or other destructive devices that will ever solve the differences of mankind. You cannot expect your neighbor to capitulate and abandon the desires of his heart just because you have a bigger club than he does. His automatic reaction will be to find a more effective weapon than you have, and soon, the original point of disagreement will be forgotten as both, you and he, scramble for superior weapons. The inevitable results of this approach should be obvious to all of us by now. Soon, all lesser points of debate fade into insignificance and the only thing that matters is "who can emerge victorious in battle."

Sadly, we have allowed ourselves to continue the stupid escalation of weaponry until we now have reached a point beyond parity, where one overzealous madman such as Hitler could put the lights out for a thousand years — or maybe forever.

I used to wonder why God warned us so often about *pride* in the teachings of the Bible. I think I understand now. It's such a short step from pride to arrogance, and from arrogance to hostility, and from hostility to battle.

Let's stop thumping our chests and baring our teeth. Or we may soon find ourselves swinging from the same vines as another species that's fond of doing those things.

The last hope of man is in the goodness of his spirit, that other great force which vies continually for his attention, and in his ability to change and adapt as he perceives errors in the direction his life is taking.

We need to stop wringing our hands in resignation. If we accept without resistance the dark, dire inevitability of worldwide destruction, we will in fact be aiding and abetting its fulfillment. A "what's the use" attitude is the greatest gift you could hand the forces of evil.

Remember who you are. You are of the family of man, created in the image of God. Your triumphs over challenges that seemed insurmountable are legendary. There is that superb, most excellent side to the spirit of man which is glimpsed only briefly under normal circumstances but springs forth boldly, valiantly, when the fates have a need for greatness.

I believe it is within the power of man to alter the frightening course that events of the past have placed him upon. But it will take a whole new outlook. A whole new attitude with which to view his former enemies.

We must begin by realizing that we have all been victims. That past and present opponents have been just as cruelly victimized as have we. That the real enemy is evil, and his henchmen are misunderstanding, lack of compassion, confusion, lack of communication, mistrust, lack of tolerance, and arrogant pride.

There has been no peace in the world for at least 45 years now. Have these constant wars solved anything? Will they ever? Of course not. The faces and the uniforms change but the battle does not. It is always pawn against pawn, and the only winner is evil.

Why can't we then recognize our common enemy, put aside our differences, and begin to focus in on the issues that *lead* men to war? Poverty, hunger, greed and all the rest. The battle must now be waged in peace, for the hearts of men. The truth is — we need each other in order to survive. We must stop hiding our heads in the sand, pretending that evil is a fantasy and Satan a figment of somebody's imagination.

We have been promised that a day will come when man will study war no more. I hope that you and I can be instrumental in bringing this about during our time. How grand it would be to have future generations refer to us as "the generation that renounced war and identified Satan as the real enemy of man."

To be sure, there will always be a carrot of temptation dangling before some jackass of a world leader who would not hesitate to plunge us all back into the abyss of despair, but if we can use our imaginations a little bit, it's fun to dream of a day when the major powers of the world will have trained themselves to be on the alert for signs of evil design from any quarter. Visualize with me a world in which reciprocal trust among nations is a standard, accepted norm. Where every proposal of good faith is not analyzed to death in a witch hunt for subversive meaning. Where men of good intent police their own attitudes to respect the rights and dreams of other men. Where one nation sees another as a true member of the family and both protect the rights of their peoples by "giving" a love of humanity, respecting the uniqueness of their neighbor.

Are we unrealistic dreamers, or do we have a right to believe that good will in the end triumph over evil? That the evil one's days are numbered because mankind has finally recognized **him** as the enemy, and has embraced brother nations in a great show of resistance to the evil design of destruction.

If, after all, the real battleground is within the hearts of men, then we must revive and study our spiritual postures. We bang on the door of rational thinking, hoping against hope that common sense will prevail. We are met instead with deceit and acts of violence that defy all logic.

We lean to our own understanding, trying to "out-think" the other fellow and wind up mired in a sea of chaotic repercussion.

We spend billions in a foolish attempt to "buy" influence, only to be rebuked by those very same nations, and then blackmailed into spending billions more.

The old ways no longer work. They were wrong to begin with and we are now reaping what we have sown.

How prophetic were the words of Albert Einstein when he said:

"The unleashed power of the atom has changed everything except our way of thinking. We shall require a substantially new manner of thinking if mankind is to survive."

In my opinion there can be no harmony of objectives between former antagonists without certain preconditions. The primary fixation for planners on both sides should be the development of a strong spirit of cooperation and forgiveness. Such a spirit demands that both parties abstain from reiterating old accusations or condemning past actions. If you begin a conference between nations by running over what you consider to be their past sins, you will be establishing a spirit of *belligerence,* not cooperation.

I was shocked recently to hear our leadership wailing away at the Soviet Union about their aggressive tendencies in certain parts of the world, just prior to the forthcoming Reagan-Gorbachev meeting.

I'm sure that some of our political planners thought that this would be a great way to put pressure on the U.S.S.R. and garner world support for our position, just before the conference. Personally I think it's stupid. If you have a disagreement with your neighbor, do you begin your discussion of the problem by bringing up all of his past mistakes, and then making sure the other neighbors hear all about it before you begin talking? Again, the focus of any conference should be upon the establishment of a workable, friendly spirit. The planners should not make a move that does not conform to this end.

Once having begun in this spirit, it is hopeful that the participants will call upon the noble side of their natures to deal with specific issues. There is no short-cut. We have been a world of suspicious travelers. The reestablishment of trust among nations will be a slow and painful process, but I think it can be done. It must be done if we are to survive.

There is another bright spot in the scheme of things. Goodness can and does spread just as easily as does evil. An attitude of cooperation and respect for other nations that do not see all things as we do, will result in a widening of our spiritual base. From that beginning, perhaps we can reverse the terrible trend that has developed over the years, and strike a balance of fairness to all.

We know the real enemy will continue to work for the total destruction of man. But knowing who he is, and what he stands for, may cause us to look beyond the surface problems for the evil influence. We have a chance. We can all help by protesting vigorously those things which we determine to be of evil origin, before they have a chance to grow.

We've patted ourselves on the back long enough now, supposing that our sophistication was equal to any problem that could arise . It isn't. We need to return to the things of the spirit — and to the giver of that spirit. Only then can we hope to aspire to human excellence.

CHAPTER NINE

YOUR ATTITUDE — YOUR AURA

Throughout the preceding pages we have been able to see that an unmistakable aura, or spiritual climate, encircles each one of us and proclaims far louder than any conscious effort on our part, just who and what we are.

It is the "whole" of our makeup and varies in brilliance, dependent upon the *attitudes* that we have accepted as part of our own sacred conclusions relevant to life.

One does not have to ponder the issue for very long in order to realize that most everyone we know or encounter, falls into one or the other of two general categories — either positive or negative.

The "attitude-aura" of the negative person will repel and resist anything new that threatens the status quo. Although negative people may often appear to be strong individuals, with a no-nonsense approach to life, they are in reality, for the most part, insecure and terribly threatened by change of any kind. Their motivations stem from a deep-seated fear of the unknown and a fervent, almost fanatic desire to preserve familiar things just as they are.

Their influence upon family members and other close associates is one of retardation. They are the dissenting voice that throws cold water upon the dreams and aspirations of all who chance to experience their negative attitude-aura.

They are easily identifiable by their lack of warmth and by their persistent attempts to belittle the efforts of others.

Most lead hapless lives in the company of those few persons they can control. New friends, business opportunities, chances for advancement, or solicitations from any quarter that suggest change, are viewed suspiciously and driven from their presence like autumn leaves before the chilly winds of winter.

There are, of course, many varied degrees of negativism ranging all the way from "sweet and frightened" to "cold and destructive," but the common bond—which you need to avoid—is rooted in "fear of all things unfamiliar" and a pitiful lack of faith in both self and deity.

The purpose of these remarks is to forearm you against attitudes of a negative vein. Perhaps to sharpen your perception as to persons in your own life who may be sapping your strength unbeknownst to you. The "attitude-aura" of which we spoke can be compared to the warm, penetrating sunlight—and to the bone-chilling subtemperatures of a cold, damp winter.

You cannot help but be affected by the atmosphere in which you spend your time. Your very thoughts will reflect the sum total of "input" from all available sources. The danger in too much exposure to negative auras should be apparent. By mental and spiritual osmosis alone, you run the risk of poisoning your own fantastic potential for great thoughts and great things.

The lesson? Avoid lengthy exposure to unhealthy attitudes lest you infect your own. Seek out and associate with strong, warm, optimistic, goal-oriented individuals who tackle each problem that comes their way with a cheerful countenance and unshakable faith in the eventual outcome.

Nothing will strengthen and nurture your **own** attitude as effectively and constructively as close association with positive people. The mere presence of strong resolve, indomitable spirit, and faithful anticipation serve to energize your self-confidence, allowing you to visualize clearly the achievement of goals dear to your heart. The more brightly optimistic you can remain, the more negative-resistant you will become. Your "attitude-aura" will then align itself with others of the "positive" world, creating yet a stronger power base for the forces of good that dare to dream of accomplishment beyond accepted limits.

In your daily activities proceed boldly, remembering your worth. The bright aura of your attitude will be visible to all, and favorable forces which you cannot suspect will be watching. The dreams of today will become the realities of tomorrow, and today's dreamers will be tomorrow's leaders.

I will act as if what I do makes a difference.
William James

You, dear reader, may one day be the hope of the world. Or perhaps your insight and empathetic nature will point the way for men to share the spirit of reason. Young man or young woman, perhaps it is **you** who carry the cure to cancer or heart disease locked away in some secret corner of your being, awaiting only the future keys of knowledge and faith to release it for the salvation of countless lives.

What mantles of greatness are waiting to be worn by worthy souls? What yet untried levels of human endeavor lie just beyond our grasp, awaiting anxiously the arrival of that one faithful explorer with the courage to venture beyond man's former boundaries. How can you suspect the true nature of your purpose here on earth if you do not permit your attitude to embrace wholeheartedly the unseen things of the spirit?

Destiny can appear to be a great snob as she weeds out pretenders to the throne of greatness, regardless of their social standing, education, or financial influence. And taps upon the shoulder some unknown person to carry the banner of new frontiers.

We are, this day, on the cutting edge of magnificent victories for the spirit of man. Like a great central broadcasting presence, the desire for world peace, tolerance for all, and mutual respect is in the air of all nations, being proclaimed by thousands of voices which grow louder each day. The need for new leadership with the ability to "feel" the spirit of mankind is urgent. The old ways are finished, and for some years now have caused us to "chug along" like an outdated vehicle with square wheels.

Old hatreds, prejudices, political decisions, and hostile attitudes have rendered the former systems obsolete and totally useless.

A completely new approach, with vigorous new leaders, is not only needed, but of necessity being shaped by the hearts of men.

Perhaps you will be one of the new leaders. As attitudes adjust and we begin to reach beyond the old borders of man's control which we established in naive belief that our intelligence alone would suffice, we will probably be surprised at how similar the "new" order of things resembles the "ancient" guidelines that God gave us in the first place.

Like children who have run away from home to avoid responsibility, we return again, with the fear of the great forest beast who nearly devoured us, fresh in our memories.

As with all concepts of change, we will need a practical starting place for the average person like you and I. I suggest we begin by cleaning up our own acts first. We have learned some important lessons from the past. Let's see that we apply them to the future.

It Begins With You

The first relationship we will need to review is perhaps the most important of them all. How do you feel about yourself?

Earlier on in this book, we looked back over our shoulders at the fading stage of "time gone by" in an effort to discover the sources of some of our beliefs, and to submerge them in the "acid test" of truth. That process is doubly important when appraising the assets and liabilities of your own character. We've talked extensively about how certain attitudes and implants could influence your life. About how you must forgive yourself, and others, in order to free your mind for thoughts of a more positive nature.

You have a program to follow in the implementation of new goals, and you know the secret of changing negative thoughts to positive thoughts.

In addition to the varied topics we've examined together in an honest exploration of the status of our attitudes, I have related to you stories from the lives of my friends, many of whom have changed completely the nature of their existence—by a change in attitude. Still, the world may believe in you, your family may expect great things of you, your friends may reinforce over and over again their faith in your eventual success, but if **you** don't believe it, it will never happen.

I have saved this particular subject for discussion until the last chapter of the book, because I want it to be fresh in your mind when you close the cover on these thoughts—perhaps for the last time.

I have observed, over the last fifty some years, a tragic illness of the spirit that comes under the heading of *"self-deception."*

It nurtures high-sounding excuses for not getting on with your plans, careers, or perhaps callings. It permits you to justify all manner of excessive preparation, time-wasting detours, or failure patterns.

It is fine to have read a book such as this one and to agree in principle with the subject matter, but it is of less value to you than a roll of toilet paper if you do not convert what you have learned to action.

The mere act of reading a book, taking a course in college, or learning a trade, does not, of and by itself, make any wheels turn.

There's a big difference in "preparing to do" and "doing."

The world needs doers, not a whole generation of people who

are "getting ready to do." You probably bought this book because the title "Attitude, The Great Life-Maker" struck a responsive cord in your mind. You have learned through your own observation that the attitudes of your contemporaries do indeed influence the quality of their lives. We are, however, not talking about "those other people." We're talking about you.

If this book has no other message, I hope it will serve to inform you that you, my friend, can be as large in life as you dare to dream, if you will only believe it. The friends I have known who have achieved success, both financial and otherwise, and yes — some have even touched greatness — were as much like you, as your next door neighbor. The only difference was in their *attitude* — about themselves.

Please take care that the realization of self-worth carries with it a complementary portion of humility. We're as good as anyone —but better than no one. With this approach to our worthiness we need not worry about "how others see us." *Reflective reaction* will take care of that for us.

History is replete with examples of how one man, or one woman, through the shining projection of an attitude, has influenced the lives of countless thousands. Let this realization become an implant in your new attitude, branded to your soul in unforgettable fashion.

One man, or one woman, can make a difference.

It has never been clear to me why the powers that control our existence seem to delight in toppling debris into the path of those souls that seem destined for greatness, some of whom have already risen from great depths of difficulty. Perhaps it has to do with the unlocking of reserves of "untapped resources." And then again, faith cannot be tested or learned where there are no obstacles.

You have certain skills, a certain manner, individual traits and viewpoints that cannot be duplicated exactly by anyone else in the world.

Most people never rise to the full potential of their being, which may very well be due to the "bed of hot coals" they must first learn to walk across before reaping the rewards of accomplishment. The majority of our fellow humans much prefer the safety of the sidelines and the relative insulation from ridicule that a middle-of-the-road approach to life seems to offer. As for you, I cannot say, but I hope this book will give you cause to reflect upon the path you have chosen, to be certain that the choice was yours, and to consider the possibility of reaching a bit higher. Your attitude is the key — your potential, unlimited.

Thoughts are the beginnings of things, but they need to undergo a conversion program before they can mature into reality. Dreams will remain dreams unless someone takes the steps necessary to give them life.

I am constantly amazed by the number of persons I meet with unfulfilled dreams. The biggest reason? They never try!

Hardly a week goes by when I am not stopped by some individual with "this great idea for a book." Some of them have new, innovative ideas of considerable merit, and I tell them so, but what happens? A month later, when our paths again cross, I ask the inevitable question, "Have you started that book yet?" The answers vary from, "No, but I'm, still thinking about it" to , "I'll get to it one of these days." In other words — no, they haven't. Others complain that they just don't know how to start. I'll tell you how. Put a piece of paper in the typewriter and write "Chapter One." Now, you've started. Don't wait until you think you've worked out every detail of your dreams before you begin them — or you will never begin. You cannot release the "tiger" of inventive genius without first unlocking the cage.

There is another common barricade that you will have to climb over in order to "get rolling." And this one probably stops more dreams in their tracks than any other. It is the well-meaning advice and subtle discouragement of family or close friends.

It goes something like this. "Hi buddy, I hear you're going to go into real estate. I hope you've got enough money to carry you through the lean times, that's a rough business." Or, "I hope you know what you're doing starting your own business. It takes a lot of know-how to make it these days." or, "I hear you're writing a book. What made you decide to do that? You're no writer. The woods are full of starving writers."

Even the good Lord, when he walked upon this earth in the person of Christ, had to put up with that kind of nonsense. It prompted him to remark that "A prophet is not without honor, except in his own home town."

The proper attitude to take in the face of this sort of deflating counsel is probably apparent to you. Don't let anybody steal your dreams.

Proceed, on course, dead ahead, and *damn the torpedoes.*

Toward Others

I have always known that our achievements, successes, financial position, or notable accomplishments, would in the final analysis, take second billing to "the way we treated others" during our lifetime.

I don't believe there is truer measure of a man, or a woman's character than that portion of their attitude which directs — or misdirects — their behavior toward other human beings. Especially significant is the position one is inclined to take in relationship to the less fortunate.

We all tend to visualize our own actions and reactions as being proper and considerate. Even so, let's mentally scan some of our "situation responses" to better understand how our attitudes can affect others.

When you find yourself in conversation with someone of slower mind than your own, are you patient and attentive, allowing them to finish their thoughts? Or do you turn away in midsentence to converse with one of your "brighter" friends?

When the "boss" walks into the room, do you rush to his side automatically, heaping smiles and glib conversation upon his head to the exclusion of everyone present? Or do you allow your friends "equal time" without resentment, or fear of being left out?

When a new employee joins the firm (or whatever,) do you hasten to make them feel welcome? Or do you "play it cool" until you know what they are up to?

If you were raised to hate Blacks, Jews, Japs, Polacks, Spiks, Dagos, Hillbillies, Yankees, Republicans, Democrats, Chinks, Krauts, Russkies, Gooneys, City Slickers, Cops, Politicians, Union Members, Nonunion Members, Square Heads, Slant Heads, Red Heads or Dead Heads: Have you confronted yourself with the fact that you were given a "negative implant" that can only produce evil? Or do you propagate the evil to future generations by repeating its theme?

When you spot someone too fat, or too skinny in your estimation, are you quick to deride that person to other people? Or perhaps to poke fun at them in a humorous way?

All of the above are examples of "poor attitude traits" and each has the potential to harm the sensibilities of one of your fellow human beings.

If you look closely, you will be able to spot an element of selfishness in each of them. Now, how can these seemingly insignificant little character traits have any effect upon the grander scheme of things in your life, or in the lives of people you know?

It is my fervent belief that the "individuals" of neighborhood, town, city, county, state, or country, are in reality the governing body in much the same way that a strong family unit contributes to the stability of a nation.

I do not believe—especially in a free society—that the tail wags the dog.

That being the case, the attitudes of these *individuals* will, given time, become the attitudes of the nation, or at least large segments of the populace. Therefore, as history has repeatedly shown, evil conspires in small groups to threaten the freedoms of a few. If it does not encounter sufficient resistance, it grows at an alarming rate until a "movement" is born.

Soon, sinister figures of the night are painting swastikas on temple doors or burning wooden crosses in the front yards of other citizens.

Recent world history should have convinced us by now that "all it takes for evil to prosper is for enough good men to do nothing."

The relevant question, the one that we have all asked ourselves is, "What can *I* do to make a difference?" The colossal scope of the world's madness alone seems to preclude any effective action by the individual — *but*, maybe that's part of the illusion. We tend to throw up our hands in helpless resignation, and by the nature of that act we add our own vote to the spirit of futility.

Maybe we have been shortchanging ourselves. Perhaps the time has come to *recognize* the great untapped power of the *individual.*

If we were to begin this day to monitor the attitudes of our chosen world leaders closely and to speak out loudly, *at once,* against injustice directed toward any group, race or individual. Who knows what we could accomplish? We would certainly challenge evil in its embryonic state instead of waiting until we had a monster to deal with. If we suffer the rights of even the tiniest minority to be impugned, we risk all that is precious to free men. If we watch silently while members of our own neighborhood are victimized, we give license to the offenders to attack us also, with little fear of justice or punishment. We need therefore to become instantly aroused at the sight of *evil intent*, whether the setting is national or local. The enemy is one and the same in both South Africa or the south side of Chicago. Injustice often appears like a small irritating infection which, if left untreated, can threaten ever growing areas of our person until in the later stages, life itself may be forfeit.

Governments, even those devoted to the best interest of their peoples, cannot be everywhere. But we, the individual citizens of the nation — and the world — **can** be. We need therefore to stamp out the brushfires of hatred and misinformation wherever they are found, before they are turned to raging infernos, consuming everything in their paths.

The world does not need a "silent majority." It cries out for the strong voices of reason and compassion, hoping, ever hoping, that its citizens will somehow find, and ascend, the brilliant, golden staircase to man's higher purpose.

Should men, I mean all men, begin to believe that their individual efforts matter. That the dignity of all, requires the protection of all. We will have conquered the spirit of helplessness, and opened the door to the widest application of peaceful restraint yet seen. It will have a price tag. Each of us, in our own sphere of influence, will be required to speak out loudly and at once, should we witness a threat to the rights of someone else. Nations composed of persons so inclined will have no mandate from their citizens to practice adventuresome excursions into territories that do not belong to them. There will be no power base from which to launch dangerous, offensive experiments against another people. Are we dreaming? Yes, we are, **but** that's the way both great and small goals are born and finally realized. We cannot solve all of the world's problems at once, but we **can** put an end to despair by doing **something.** The great weight of the world's true, heartfelt desires are with us. Let us begin.

Preparing The Young

As we send our young people into the world, let us determine that they will go forward from our positions without the handicap of "faulty input."

Let's teach them to relish the truth. To diligently search out the hidden motives behind each proposition that comes their way. Prepare them to question authority. To weigh each decision with an awareness of how it will affect others.

Schooling should contain classes dealing with the proper formulation of their attitudes along the guidelines we discussed earlier in these pages. If the fresh, new, energetic minds of our upcoming generations can contain an automatic reverence for the rights of others; a sincere tolerance for viewpoints different from their own; the flexibility to enlist the ingredients of fair play; and mutual compromise into those areas of disagreement which require a "largeness" on the part of both sides, then perhaps we will truly begin to move toward that higher plateau of human existence which we all seek.

Instead of training our young to doggedly pursue their own goals with little or no concern for the wishes of others where conflict appears, let's teach them to expertly search out the hallowed middle ground that will be the best course of action for both sides.

Our indoctrination starting from "day one" has always been to "win" at whatever task we put our hand to. Winning is fine, and should be encouraged, in certain competitive situations. On the other hand, nobody wins when one group of people profits at the expense of another, or when a race, religion, or class of people is made to suffer because of unfair advantage by an indifferent majority.

We're leaving out terribly important aspects of human conduct when we teach winning at any price, no matter the impact upon those who do not, or cannot win. Somehow we need to inject into our instructive procedures a temperate measure of moral responsibility. There can never be a meeting of the minds, a joining of the spirits, in any contested area of human endeavor where one faction is forced to accept conditions which they know to be unfair. Inequitable or obstructionist tactics, in the long run, win nothing. There remains in effect an unwritten law of reciprocal retribution; a polarizing pendulum of fair play which will not suffer the victims of life to remain unavenged.

As tempting as momentary advantage may appear to be, the price to be paid is far too high. It turns out to be true that both nations and individuals who "sow the wind" inevitably "reap the wild wind."

It may strike you as almost academic in nature, this obvious need for an effective counter-balance between "prizes sought" and "quarter given."

Surely, we say to ourselves, mankind by reason of his magnanimous nature will grope exhaustively for reasonable and just disposition of debatable issues.

Such is not the case.

By default, the prevailing attitudes which deal with man's sense of fair play were left to, and supposedly nurtured by, religious instruction.

We really have no "code of conduct" which all men are expected to abide by because it isn't taught to us other than through the medium of religion.

The problem here of course is that not all men adhere to religious training. Many have no religion at all. Many others pay only token respect to their religious affiliation, and countless thousands strive endlessly to twist doctrine to their own advantage.

Religion is, after all, nothing more than man's interpretation of his relationship with his God. Beyond that, it is utilized all too often as a reason for strife between Arab and Jew, Moslem and

Christian, Russian and American, and so on. God did not intend it to be so.

The rules of conduct must be reasoned out during the formative years and must be based upon the principle that we deserve no more than we are willing to give. Without invoking the conflicting elements of various religious orders, we can establish guidelines, the foundations of which are rooted in all faiths that recognize a supreme being, and yet are offensive to none.

That "new way of thinking" mentioned by Einstein must contain as one of its primary ingredients a universally acknowledged recognition that we are **accountable** for our actions. With this premise, perhaps we can move forward together in mutual respect and harmony.

Of Things Bright and Beautiful

In much the same way that a surgeon is called upon to slice through healthy tissue in order to expose a diseased, life-threatening cancerous growth, I have, at points throughout this book, found it necessary to disturb areas of our attitudes that may, long ago, have been relegated to semiprecious status in our memories.

Moreover, we have had to look closely at *negative growth-patterns* in an effort to sharpen our eyes to recognize evil and evil intent.

But the real message at the heart of these observations is one of hope. Of great faith in the spiritual side to man's nature and a fervent longing to witness, first hand, during my lifetime and yours, the decisive victory of all men over the destructive tendencies thrust upon them by the master of deceit.

I believe, as I have stated before, that we are now on the threshold of a great new plateau of human awareness.

Our young college students, many of whom I have occasion to

associate with, are among the brightest that this nation has ever produced. They are, for the most part, more emotionally advanced for their years than were their earlier counterparts. They are not so quick to jump at every new notion that they are exposed to during the course of their studies. And they do question, thank God, theory and practice of not only established educational procedures, but beyond that also to the inquisition of so-called experts.

They want to know "where this guy is coming from." They are not content to accept the thoughts of someone else as being correct, without "testing" them against their own measurements of credibility. That's great news for all of us. It means they cannot be led around by the nose, and that they will be one tough group to persuade when the issue involves jeopardizing the rights of someone else.

Also on the cheerier side are the almost daily announcements of bold new advances in worldwide communications. It will not be so easy for large blocks of our fellow humans to be misled through the manipulation of information. Furthermore, citizens of other nations are beginning to **demand** full disclosure. The stakes have become far too high to rely solely upon the good graces of some government as the only source of enlightenment.

Another area in which there glimmers a spark of hopeful encouragement is the highly competitive field of "world transportation". Distances have dramatically been reduced to mere hours of flight time to any destination you might choose to visit. Competition between the "people movers" of all major powers has driven the cost of getting from here to there steadily downward. Social pressure will ultimately force stricter countries to relax their visa requirements and eventually, as time goes by, to encourage the influx of visiting tourists. As exchanges between differing cultures increase, common ground can more easily be found upon which to build firmer friendships.

As the old hard-line thinkers are slowly replaced by the new vitality of younger leaders, trust, once again can be earned between great peoples. But it can never endure where we permit the "gloom and doomers" to dredge up past sins to shake before our noses as we struggle to restore confidence between great powers. There is no earthly gain to be realized by sifting through the ashes of follies past. It's hard — very hard — to forgive and forget. But we may as well face the truth right now. There can be no new beginnings until we are willing to let go of the past. It helps somewhat to realize that where nations (ours and theirs) have imposed their presence and influence upon smaller countries, it was almost always because of a defensive fear. If trust can again be restored, if new leadership attuned to the spiritual longings of man can be found, and if the individuals of each nation will by the strength of their numbers make known their presence and their desires, perhaps then the custodians of their governments will comprehend the often forgotten truth that they are merely caretakers.

The great mass of millions who inhabit a nation are the true owners. When the governments no longer reflect the desires of their people, they forfeit the right to represent them.

Strange as it may sound, there is another progression which is in the best interest of the world in general. It is to be found in the attitude taken by the citizens of all the earth's countries, pertaining to propaganda.

Like a young lad who runs away to join the circus — reality teaches a certain insight. The glitter, glamour and hyperbolic hoopla of the big-top in no way resembles the hard work, constant travel, and rigid training schedules that are required to maintain the shiny face of entertainment shown to the world. So it is with most of us who have been around for awhile. We have learned to "discount," just as our young runaway has, certain items that are contrived to mislead, exaggerate, or influence our thinking, particularly in the field of politics. The rest of the world, I assure you, has learned to do the same thing. The implication here is that we no longer "buy" everything that's fed to us, at face value. The new plateau of human awareness of which I spoke earlier is making it harder and harder for governments or deceitful leaders to "pull off" accusations which have no basis in truth. And to that I say — let's make them prove every damn word.

There slowly emerges, from the total assembly of thoughts here, a clear-cut challenge to all of us. We each, in our own way, in our own portion of life, must try to restore faith to the thoughts of man.

We live in a world where it becomes increasingly more difficult to depend upon anything. Over a period of time we have calloused our minds against great expectations. We need to be individual examples of solid dependability, of optimistic outlook, and to regain once more a strong belief in our abilities, our God given right to influence — at least in part — the direction and the maturity of our own destinies.

Man is a two-part creation consisting of both body and spirit. He has, unfortunately, stressed the physical care and comfort of his body, while all but ignoring the spiritual strengths of his character.

The results are to be seen in most of the "Unsolvable" problems we are faced with today. Teenage drug addiction for example cannot be effectively dealt with by the mere threat of punishment, loss of health, or loss of self-esteem. The strength to effectively combat monsters of this size must come from a source far greater than mere physical desire to overcome.

The same is true of teenage crime, teenage prostitution, teenage suicide, and murder. They're all related — they're all evidence of bankrupt spiritual strength.

And the adult population? We build magnificent machines to calculate, to travel into space, to prolong a fading life — and to destroy. We do all of these things with no input, no influence, no considerations from the spiritual side of our natures. Result? We have become hostages of our own ingenuity. And we are now in a race of sorts to awaken man to his spiritual strengths — before it's too late.

The restoration of faith, both in God and self, is the first step, the initial dependency needed, to arouse within our breast that forgotten essence of our being. That miraculous, magical, indescribable something that warms by its presence, and can be seen in brightness of eye and quickness of step.

Confidence follows faith, refusing to bend before the insurmountable. Eager to contend with challenge and courageous at points of decision.

Who among us has not witnessed the determined spirit at work in its host body. It becomes the driving force, the irrepressible battering ram against resistance, able always to circumvent the most stubborn of obstacles. What worthier goal? What more meaningful challenge than to aid in restoring this spark of the fullness of life to those we love? We can do it you know! We can begin by attacking each negative thought we encounter. By uplifting the spirits of our downtrodden friends and letting them know, unmistakably, that we have every confidence in them and that they must also be strong in faith. By this act of giving alone, we will strengthen our own spirits and ultimately charge the particles of self-assurance of each life we touch.

What attitude could possibly be complete without a strong desire to be of use to loved ones? The day of the individual is here. Governments will not solve the everyday problems of our lives. In fact, there is some doubt as to whether they will be able to solve *any* of our problems. We may have to do that ourselves. In any case, it becomes clearer by the day that the strength of a people — must come from the people, and that by way of their spiritual fibre.

We have a debt. More than that — we have a sacred trust. If you wonder about the accuracy of that statement, do this thing for me.

When next you pick up that infant son, or daughter, or grandchild, look closely, really closely, at the innocence in those bright young eyes. When you carry that sleepy little warm body to bed at night held tightly against your own, and you tuck him or her cozily into their soft nest of brightly colored blankets, pause for a moment. Watch as the beautiful little eyelashes flicker slowly to a close like tiny butterflies coming to rest. Touch gently the soft cheek, the unruly hair, the perfect features of that darling face. Smell the freshness, the pureness, of a life yet to be lived.

And tremble.

Feel the prayer rise within your soul as the small chest heaves easily up and down in deep, trusting sleep.

Oh Lord. Bless this little one. Grant that the world in which this child will live and grow can somehow rid itself of hatred and greed and the horrors of war. Let the attitudes of men and nations reflect a newness of purpose. A tolerance of one another. A fairness of spirit. Give me the vision, the insight, to do all that I can in harmony with other members of my generation, so that the legacy we leave behind for this child — all children — will be one of joyful self-discovery through the enrichment of other lives. When I instruct this young, pliable mind entrusted to my care, guide me in shaping an attitude based upon truth, without evil prejudice or haughty manner.

In the world of the future Lord, let there be freedom from fear, freedom from suspicion, and a compelling spiritual craving to remedy the needs of all the earth's peoples.

Let there be laughter, compassion, and happiness. But above all — let there be love.

Oh dear God — let there be love.

THE END